"What happens when an amazing humanitarian meets a dedicated artist? It's the beginning of *A Wondrous Journey*. In a world of strife and suffering here is a story that must be read and emulated. Dr. "Bobby" MacGuffie is a sublime heroine who simply says "I will do my best" and Lynn Manzione simply says "And I will make the world aware". If they do not inspire you it's likely you are not alive—but if you want to live again...READ THIS BOOK!!! Thank you Bobby & Lynn and peace to you both."

—Malachy McCourt, Actor and Author

"This book should be a part of the education system. The messages are ones that could benefit anyone who has ever struggled."

—Mikhail Baryshnikov, Dancer, Author and Actor

"Dr. Martha MacGuffie proves that one person can make a difference in this world! The impact she has made in the lives of thousands is a legacy for us all."

—Leila and Bob Macauley, Founders of AmeriCares

"Martha MacGuffie is living proof that regardless of age or hardship, the human spirit is indomitable, and can achieve anything it sets its sights on."

—Ellen Burstyn, Actor and Author

"To fully understand the grand work of Dr. Martha MacGuffie is to appreciate it in the context of her extraordinary personal hardship and heartache. Here is a hero's story."

—Scott Vanderhoef, Rockland County Executive

"It is with a great deal of pleasure that I offer a glowing testimonial for this book."

—Benjamin A. Gilman, Former Congressman
CEO, The Gilman Group

"We can all find inspiration in the story of these two great women. A big thank you to both of them for bringing these messages to the world."

—Darlene Gudrie Butts, Author and Motivational Speaker

A Wondrous Journey

a small book *with* big lessons

A Wondrous Journey

a small book *with* big lessons

Dr. Martha MacGuffie
& Lynn Cluess Manzione

www.lynnmanzione.com

awondrousjourneybook@gmail.com

ISBN - 9781976139772

Cover Design and Typeset by Melanie Shellito

Printed in the United States of America

*This book is dedicated to the purpose of living life
to its fullest and to the memory of Reid, Rob, and Scott
who never had the chance to.*

Contents

to start

It is not always clear at the start of an experience what its actual purpose is but given time it all comes into focus. For me, and the particular experience that I am referring to, the start was a simple bike ride. My intended purpose for the ride was twofold; to alter my ordinary routine (I was in a rut) and to lose weight (I had come to own twenty pounds more than I wanted). The end result was two years spent writing this book, a treasured friendship with the person that inspired me to do so, and unexpected moments of self-discovery along the way.

As a bonus, I did lose the weight, and oddly it only took that one ride and the eight weeks of sitting on the couch that followed to get me to where I wanted to be—twenty-two pounds lighter than my pre-ride weight. I know that sounds impossible but that's what having your jaw wired shut for eight weeks can do for you. It can also do a fairly good job of altering the ordinary. In case there is any confusion … I crashed my bike that day. The series of events that led up to the crash could not have been better orchestrated. I coasted towards an intersection, stood up to stretch my legs, looked both ways to check for traffic, gently squeezed the brakes in case I needed to stop, missed seeing the large pothole that my front tire was headed towards, hit the pothole, locked up on my brakes, flew over the handle bars and landed on my face. There was substantial damage. Specifically, a jaw dislocated and broken in three places, nine broken teeth (which led to a year's worth of weekly dental appointments) and a jagged cut on my chin that required a plastic surgeon to return my face to its previous condition.

That is just the physical account of what I went through after my bike ride. There was other stuff that came up as a result of the unpleasant downtime. On top of feeling physically rotten, I found the eight-week-mouth-wired-shut period allowed for me to feel emotionally rotten as well. The good news was I had come upon some spare time, and since those feelings were there and I was not doing much else—I figured I might as well deal with them.

I guess part of what I faced during that recuperation time was typical for my age. I was forty-six years old, primed and ready for that midlife thing. But this went even deeper than that. I had always felt that I had missed out on something, and for quite some time I had been regretfully sitting on the fact that I had never followed either of the career paths I had dreamed up for myself in my younger days. Yes, I had become a photographer (one of my dreams), but not the kind I had wanted to be. From the age of nine when I received my first Instamatic camera for Christmas, I had thoughts of being a world traveling photojournalist—my inspiration being Jacques Cousteau and *National Geographic* magazine. I loved them both for bringing the unseen and unknown to the masses. Then later, when I found out that I was better at getting my thoughts on paper than I was at getting them past my lips, I thought it could be great fun to be a writer. I even had a high school teacher encourage me in that direction once, but since she was my basketball coach and not my English teacher, I never felt compelled to run out and act on her suggestion. As it turned out, it was my lack of self-confidence that made my decision for me—I didn't follow either dream. Instead, I let life take me where it would—to over two decades worth of portraits, weddings, and bar mitzvahs. What had happened was easy to figure out—dreams don't turn into reality unless they are followed by the actions that are required to bring them to life. Coming to terms with this was not helping me feel any better.

During the time that I was recovering, I spent a good number of hours on my couch with the television being my companion of choice. Having cut back significantly on conversation because of the wires that were keeping my teeth clenched shut, I had a lot of time to think about the regrets I had been carrying around. My frame of mind, paired with my ravenous hunger, made this one of the most unpleasant times of my life. Everything seemed to irritate me. The endless stories that were being played on my television screen were no exception. It was the hour of undoing of beautiful young celebrity women. All of whom seemed to be simultaneously falling apart in the public eye; or maybe it was because of the public eye. They were women who were shaving their heads and clubbing cars with baseball bats. They were women being sent off to jail in designer clothing. They were women caught up in custody battles over children that obviously were not top priority. I found it disturbing that they were the women we were being forced to focus on. I was pretty sure there were others that were much more deserving of our attention. Annoyed at the media and irritated with myself, I had one of those light bulb moments. With the realization that I was not getting any younger and that I was dissatisfied with how my career had gone so far, I decided the time had come to take the action I should have taken so many years before. The time had come for me to get to a place that more closely resembled the career I had wanted, or, at the very least, make an attempt at it.

Right then, as my television broadcast its definition of what it meant to be beautiful and successful, I made a decision to try to do something to bring out a more truthful description of what beauty and success looks like. I signed up for a class at the International Center For Photography (ICP) called Long Term Project and headed off to my first class with a loosely put together thought for a book. It was to be a collection of photographs and essays featuring a number of women who I believed better represented the word beautiful. I envisioned them being defined by how they lived their lives, rather than how they looked, what designer labels they wore, or who they ran with. My plan was simple—find them, contact them, photograph them, and write about what made them fit my definition of beauty.

Although this was not completely thought out, I had already decided on my first subject; she was a woman doctor who lived in my hometown. From what I had read in the local papers over the years, I knew she was a well-respected surgeon, and somewhat of a celebrity in our area because of the humanitarian work she had been doing in Africa. I couldn't have asked for it to be more convenient. Fired up by my new mission, I sent her a letter asking if she would be interested in my project and planned to follow that up with a call a week later.

One week later I was on my way into the city for my class; I was stuck in traffic on the George Washington Bridge and I knew I had to have my next step accomplished before I walked into my classroom. It was time. I picked up my cell phone and dialed Dr.

MacGuffie's number. As the phone rang, I started hoping for an answering machine. I started wondering what I thought I was doing and who I thought I was in trying to put my opinion out there—for at least a sliver of the world to hear. What had gotten into me? For the past forty-six years I had been comfortable with following my routine from the day before ... what was this sudden need to break that cycle? I felt an urge to hang up the phone and forget the whole idea. Instead, a woman's voice greeted me with a hello. "Hello, Dr. MacGuffie?" I inquired.

"Yes," she answered.

"My name is Lynn Cluess Manzione, I sent you a letter last week ..."

"Oh yes," she replied. "You're the one writing the book about women."

In that moment it became official—there was no turning back, I *was* the one writing the book about women. "Yes," I said, trying to sound as if that was something I had to answer every day. "Do you think you would be interested in participating in the project?" Her answer surprised me.

"I'm sorry," she said, "I don't have any money to put into your project."

It wasn't in an irritated way. She sounded apologetic. Suddenly I became aware that this woman was sought after; that she had been approached a time or two before for assistance in one cause or another. Based on my personal history I would have normally thanked her for her time and packed in the whole idea, but because she seemed genuinely sorry that she had to decline, I got the feeling that I should put myself out there for another attempt.

"I don't want your money," I assured her. "What I want is to tell your story." After a bit more explaining, she agreed to my request for a meeting and we decided on the following Sunday morning.

That Sunday morning was the first of what quickly became many, and before long the Sundays were mixed in with every other day of the week. In a short space of time I became a regular at Dr. MacGuffie's, and in listening to her stories, it became evident that I had stumbled upon the perfect example of a life lived beautifully. Although it was a life that seemed to be both blessed and cursed, it was one that was filled with purpose, and for me the purpose of an experience was coming into focus.

Through stories from Dr. MacGuffie's life, this journey has easily accomplished my original mission to show that beauty is heart and soul deep—it also offered many surprise extras that came as a bonus. One of those added benefits: my own moments of self-discovery as a result of time spent with an incredibly inspiring woman.

we meet

After I had set my first appointment to meet with Dr. MacGuffie, I figured I had better get on the Internet and do a little research. I sat down at my computer, googled her, and found out some pretty interesting things. First of all, she was eighty-two years old, and as far as I could tell, she was still practicing medicine. The Internet also told me that Dr. MacGuffie and Dr. Renée M. Brilliant, a pediatric hematologist, had started a non-profit organization called SHARE, in 1987. I was feeling energized—Dr. MacGuffie was perfect for my project! According to their website, SHARE, which is the acronym for Society of Hospital and Resources Exchange, "consists of doctors, nurses, paramedics, business, and lay people who volunteer their time to work together toward a common goal to help children and communities in Kenya, Africa." I was excited about meeting her. I picked up a few more details about SHARE and moved off of their website and started reading through some of the endless articles I had found online about her.

What I learned from those articles left me very aware that my bike ride had somehow landed me exactly where I was supposed to be ... at the doorstep of a woman who truly deserved our attention. The articles that I read through that day introduced me to a person who epitomized what my project was about. They told of a woman that had broken through the societal boundaries of her day by becoming the first woman surgeon to come out of Columbia Medical School. Those articles I came upon about Dr. Martha MacGuffie informed me that she became the first woman doctor on staff at the New York hospital where she spent fifty years building her reputation as the hospital's most sought-after reconstructive surgeon. The articles also told me that all of this occurred while she was raising her eight children—five daughters and then finally three sons. And as if all of this was not enough to solidify my desire to tell her story, those articles told me that this woman had also lost those three sons. Because of that unbelievably tragic experience, Dr. MacGuffie found a way to use her grief as the fuel to move forward in her drive to help others.

It was in the early 1980s that Dr. MacGuffie realized that the disease that had claimed the lives of her two youngest boys, Reid and Rob, might not have been as it originally seemed. Rob and Reid had both been born with a genetic blood disorder known as Fanconi's anemia. It was a disease that required frequent transfusions, and when the symptoms that her boys began having in their teenage years began to change, Dr. MacGuffie was faced with an outcome that had little chance of turning out well. At first she was simply caught up in the desperate experience of running them from specialist to specialist, trying to find out what it was that was causing such a devastating turnaround in their condition. Then when it was apparent that there would be no stopping the decline, she faced the task of figuring out how to deal with her pain while at the same time witnessing the toll it was taking on the rest of her family. The quickness of it all left no chance of constructing a logical understanding of what was happening to her boys. It hit Reid first, and then within a year Rob. The process of watching them die was numbing and the experience surreal. It was only after the reality of their deaths had settled in that she began to look at the why. What she came to see was the close relationship of the symptoms her boys had suffered to the symptoms that were suddenly and mysteriously claiming the lives of so many in that decade. Those symptoms were the symptoms of AIDS in the early 1980s. When she discovered that some of the transfusions her boys had been given came from Rikers Island inmates, a large population of men who were dying from this new disease, she understood the disease that really claimed her boys was AIDS. In time she would figure out how to deal with all of this. In time her response would be to go where AIDS was having the most devastating effect and figure out what she could do about it, and so SHARE was born.

After processing all of this information, all I could think was how courageous this woman was. I knew I was about to meet an extraordinary person. Based on my findings, I had a clear picture as to what my interview with Dr. MacGuffie would be about: AIDS, her boys, and how she found the strength to do what she was doing in Africa. I walked in her front door that first Sunday with my questions all typed out and my camera at the ready. The story was already written in my head. Simply put, it would pretty much regurgitate everything that was already written about her ... at least that was my plan.

When I entered her kitchen, where we would sit for our interview, I immediately noticed the articles, pictures, and notes she had spread all over the table. Dr. MacGuffie had some research of her own going on. The first words out of her mouth were, "We have to save Lake Victoria!" Number one, I had no idea what or where Lake Victoria was, number two, I didn't have a clue what was wrong with Lake Victoria or why it needed saving, and number three, I was not sure that given the previous two problems I was going to be of any use being part of the solution. Not wanting to sound like a complete idiot, I stood there, awkwardly silent. I'm pretty sure that instead of sounding like a complete idiot I more than likely looked like one!

Lynn Cluess Manzione

As our conversation continued, it was becoming evident that Dr. MacGuffie wanted to talk about something other than what I had planned. I tried to redirect the interview back to the questions I wanted answered, which were questions about her. Despite my diligent efforts, Dr. MacGuffie was on to a chemical compound that she was concerned was causing high rates of cancer in the Lake Victoria region, which by then I had found out, was the area in Kenya where she had worked for over twenty years.

Towards the end of our time that day we did get around to some of the personal stuff that she had gone through with her boys. As we walked through her home she showed me the endless number of photographs of her family that were sprawled across every open surface. They were a group of people she was obviously quite proud of. "I have five daughters," she told me. "Each one is either a doctor or a teacher," she said as a smile spread across her face. As Dr. MacGuffie showed me around her home, I photographed her and got a bit of history on her time there—almost fifty years.

The end of my visit that first day gave me a clear indication of who this woman was and what people thought of her. As we walked around her property, Dr. MacGuffie and I were suddenly overwhelmed by the strong odor of natural gas. In mid-sentence she sprung into action—I found out that a doctor who has spent fifty years dealing with the aftermath of explosions, fires, and burns will do that when faced with the possibility of it happening again. Suddenly my forty-six-year-old legs were picking up the pace, trying to keep up with her eighty-two-year-old legs. She quickly climbed her front steps and called the fire department. Within minutes there were two truckloads of firemen spread out across her property. When their job was done, and it was discovered that the odor was coming from work that was being done down the road, the firemen surrounded the doctor and asked me if they could have their picture taken with her. As I rounded the guys together for their photo-op with Dr. MacGuffie, she said, "Wait—I'll be right back, I need to go get my honorary fire chief hat." With her wearing her chief hat and the guys wearing proud smiles, I captured an image that revealed the deep respect that was present. It not only showed me how much admiration they had for her, but also how much she had for them. After hearing stories of the burn cases she has treated over her fifty-year career, it is easy to understand why. When they drove away she looked at me and shaking her head she said, "They run into burning buildings and save people's lives. I always wonder how a person develops that kind of courage and character. They truly are heroes." I agreed, and while I stood there feeling minuscule with my camera draped around my neck, I couldn't help but wonder if she realized the strength of her own character and how much of a hero she was.

Lynn Cluess Manzione

the purpose

A few weeks after I photographed Dr. MacGuffie I was asked to do an exhibit of my photography at our local library. I suggested that it be on the body of work I had on the doctor. The woman who ran the exhibits was thrilled with the idea and suggested we do it for Women's History month, which was several months away. After giving it some thought, I decided instead of an exhibit of stills, I should do a documentary to highlight the doctor's inspiring life. With that as my goal I was back to Dr. McGuffie's, Bobby as I was now calling her—a nickname given to her by her father as a young girl, and the name she prefers. Settling into an office in Bobby's house, I began collecting stories and photographs that spanned from her childhood through present day. Along with the endless number of photographs were folders filled with articles and records of all of the awards she has won through the years. The more I read through those articles the more I was convinced that the world really needed to know Bobby MacGuffie. I was also convinced that the book I should write and would write would be her story—the story of Dr. Martha MacGuffie. I realized this change would result in a bigger undertaking than my original plan, one I wasn't even sure I could pull off, but I was suddenly aware that I was in a position to rewind time and go after something I was too afraid to try all those years ago.

During one of my visits to Bobby's to work on the documentary, I got up the nerve to ask her if we could write her story together. I told her that I wanted to put my original project aside for now, because I felt her story was too large to be a snippet in a collection of stories. Thankfully she agreed, and before I knew it we began working together almost daily. With each story Bobby shared, my admiration for her increased, and strangely so did my questions for myself. I started wondering what I might have accomplished if I had the kind of drive and fearlessness that Bobby had. When the day came to show the documentary at the library there wasn't an open seat available. We had to do a second showing to accommodate the number of people that had come. When the program was over, Bobby was surrounded by a large number of people that had come to tell her stories of how she had touched their lives. They wanted to thank her for all she had done, show their respect for her. I had never seen such a public outpouring of love. Those same people were coming up to me and telling me that I needed to get the documentary out into schools, that it was inspiring, that there were so many positive messages in it for kids. The thought of using Bobby's story as a way to motivate and inspire kids was absolutely something I was interested in, and the messages were definitely ones that would have made a difference in the direction I took my life had I heard them when I was younger. I couldn't help but think that I might not have had any regrets had I learned the lessons that Bobby's story offered before so many years had passed. The good news was that I was learning them now and I was feeling that feeling again. I had somehow landed just where I needed to be. I was starting to feel really grateful for potholes.

Within a few weeks we did start going around to schools with the documentary, and the reactions from the students allowed me to see the positive impact that it was having. I was more than thrilled to be a part of it and I could not help thinking how lucky I was to be working with Bobby in getting her life's valuable lessons out to children at such an important time in their development. The kids were so responsive to Bobby's story, and based on the questions they were asking, it was obvious they were connecting to the lessons that were being offered. Lessons that come from the principles Bobby has lived by. Lessons that they can take forward and use to get them through the inevitable challenges they will face in their own lives. Lessons I will be taking forward in mine.

Lynn Cluess Manzione

lesson one

Lynn Cluess Manzione

you can achieve most anything

"You can achieve most anything if you want it badly enough and are willing to work hard enough."

—Dr. Robert N. MacGuffie

The **quote that heads this chapter** is something that Bobby's father always told her and something she believes firmly in. Her belief comes from the fact that she is living proof of its truth. She figured out what she wanted in life, decided she would do whatever she needed to make it happen and then she did the work that was required. It was as simple as that.

My experience differed. I did none of those things. I shied

away from what I wanted in life, decided it would be impossible to achieve and therefore did nothing to try to make it happen. I was living proof that if you do nothing to go after your dream, it will not appear. I was curious to know how a person like Bobby takes shape. I wanted to know where that level of drive comes from and how I could get me some. I asked Bobby how she thought she came to be the person that she is. The following story from Bobby offers some insight into that.

Bobby on being who you are ...

I have a recollection of what is probably my earliest memory. In it, I am sitting at the bottom of a flight of stairs leading from a room my family is staying in while vacationing in the country. It is a perfect place. There is a trail that leads off into the woods just steps from where I am sitting. The trail is dusty and dirty and it leads into a forest that gets darker and cooler the further in you go. The woods are where I feel most at ease and I love to spend my time there with nature all around me. It's captivating watching all the different animals that live there; they fascinate me. The forest is where I was headed before being distracted by something in my peripheral vision. It is a large toad and now it is in my hands. I am inspecting it, thoroughly taken by its odd flecks of color and the texture of its bumpy skin. I sit back down and take in everything about this creature. We are face to face giving each other the once over. He is a pleasant surprise and I decide I will take this new friend on the adventure I am about to go on. Up I get and off we go, down the dusty trail. While most of the other people are off doing one of the things the resort arranges for its guests, I am alone with a frog on my way into the woods and not only am I happy about it, it is what I prefer.

This was fairly typical of my social preferences in my early years. Animals, nature, solitude—if I had all three at once, it was a perfect world. The thing that I recall most about my childhood is that I always felt different from the other girls my age, even my own sisters. My older sister Jane and my younger sister Ann were very much alike. They were good daughters, good sisters, and good girls. They fit flawlessly with the world and were very happy. I was a contrarian, a tomboy and a misfit and I wasn't at all interested in the things that normal girls were interested in. I liked climbing trees, the outdoors and animals. Even animals that normal girls found revolting—like snakes, mice, and rats. Typically, I didn't like any of the things that I should have, and I liked all of the things that I shouldn't. I was confused and felt like an oddity. Because of that, I found it easier to spend my time with animals. Animals didn't notice that I was different, and they didn't try to change me.

I think it was very difficult for my mother being that I was not a typical girl. She was not able to connect with me, and feeling the differences between us, I could not connect with her either. She would try by buying outfits or other items, and I would refuse to wear them. Baggy clothes were my preference. I preferred cutoff shorts and loose shirts and anything she picked out was sure to cause a meltdown on my part. I think that hurt her, and it put a distance between us. I remember watching how she would interact with my sisters and I would feel left out, but I knew I didn't belong there. I wished I could be like her though, she was very well liked and involved with humanitarian work and I admired that. I do remember that my father was crazy about her and that the love and respect my parents had for each other was obvious. I found that comforting.

Though my mother and I had an awkward relationship, my father was someone that I felt a strong connection to. I admired him and was very aware of the satisfaction and respect his work as a physician and surgeon brought him. I wanted that too. I think I knew from the age of five that I wanted to be a doctor. I loved how he interacted with his patients and his caring way. My father began taking me on rounds with him when I was very young. I don't think he could help it—I would follow him everywhere and pester him until he gave in. He was very accommodating though, and his patients didn't seem to mind. As I got older my visits with him included time in the operating room and I saw things that were not at all normal for a child to see. I saw births and deaths, amputations, disease, and surgeries. I guess that was unusual, but I loved it—and my father knew how much his allowing it meant to me.

Although my mother was not crazy about my interest in the medical field, my father encouraged it, even though careers of that kind were not at all what women were preparing for in those days. And though it was not the attitude of society at the time, my father believed that women should have the same opportunities as men. Because of his mind-set and the fact that I loved everything about science and the medical field, becoming a doctor was never anything I felt beyond my reach—even though everyone else felt it was.

If I had to figure out what it was that gave me the resolve to go after being a doctor, it would probably be that when I spent that time with my father, I felt my happiest. I found the science of medicine interesting and I felt good when I was seeing the difference my father could make in a person's life. Also, I didn't feel that I fit in anywhere else as much as I did there—and I didn't think I should try to make myself fit in somewhere else just because it was more socially acceptable. I had such a good feeling about being in that setting that I just figured it was something I should do.

dissimilar similarities

Listening to Bobby tell this story brought back memories of my own childhood. I was a tomboy too. I was most happy while out and about looking for adventure, or while quietly sitting in my father's workshop, watching him bring new things to life from neatly stacked piles of lumber. I loved being with my father while he worked on his projects and eventually I took on my own. Like the collection of wooden rubber-band-firing guns that I made for all of the kids in the neighborhood so that our war games would seem more realistic. That was not something my older sisters were doing but it made me happy. Besides being a novice woodworker, I also enjoyed contests of any kind—on whatever playing field was available. Whether it was someone's backyard baseball field, or the school's football field, or a neighbor's basketball court—it didn't matter what the game was—as long as there was competition. The more Bobby and I talked, the more I was finding it strange that even though I had always been comfortable with competition on the playing field, I shied away from it when it came to going after what I wanted in life. There I played it safe. Obviously, that was not Bobby's philosophy.

From an early age Bobby brushed aside improbability and followed her dream despite many people telling her it would be an impossible one to achieve. She also allowed herself to be different. That might sound trivial, but it is a defining moment. When you are a kid it can be easier to go along with what everyone else is doing rather than what feels right to you. Bobby would not settle for that and she stepped outside of what was acceptable for young girls in her day. By doing that she became one of the women that made it easier for the next generation of women to be what they wanted. I guess being a child of the sixties and seventies, where I witnessed first-hand the changes the women of that day were going through, it really impressed me that Bobby had been so far ahead of that transformation. My conversations with Bobby were starting to evolve into a quest for self-discovery. I wanted to figure out why I hadn't done the same. Although the road was not yet smoothly paved when it was my time to choose a career, the women of Bobby's generation (and those that followed in the sixties and seventies) had certainly cleared the path. We were much better situated to go after the careers of our dreams. Suddenly I was feeling guilty. Why hadn't I become an oceanographer or writer or photojournalist? It would have been so much easier for me than it was for Bobby!

What came up when I asked those questions of myself were memories of a few conversations that had taken place when I was a child. The first was with a teacher to whom I had confided that I might want to be an oceanographer. That reveal came in third grade, when I was asked by that teacher to stay behind while the rest of my classmates headed off to the lunchroom. I was sure that my detainment had to do with my less than stellar performance on the previous day's math test. I was happily surprised when my teacher asked me to stay and have lunch with her instead. When she started our conversation with a question that led me to believe that she thought of me as more than a struggling math student ... I was thrilled. "Lynn," she began, "what is it that you think you might like to be when you grow up?" My first reaction to her question was relief; then, I felt flattered. Obviously, this teacher was taking an interest in my future because she saw something special in me, I thought. I wasn't there to get lectured on my lack of interest in division and multiplication! Feeling much more relaxed then when I was first asked to stay behind, I told my teacher that I thought I wanted to study ocean life and photograph it for the rest of the world to see. (I loved watching Jacques Cousteau specials, had just gotten a Kodak Instamatic camera for Christmas, and had spent a day out of our Easter vacation at Sea World in Florida where I photographed Flipper, the star of my favorite television show!) I was actually excited to share this information with my teacher. Her answer to my excitement was, "Well, that may be hard for you since you need to be really good at math to be an oceanographer." BAM! How did I not see that coming? I'm sure her comment was a clever attempt to encourage me to improve my grades. Instead, what it did was completely shut me down—I never had another thought of being an oceanographer again. On top of that, it didn't motivate me to take an interest in arithmetic!

The next conversation I recalled while I strolled down Bad Memory Lane occurred when I was in high school. I had just gotten a 35 mm camera and I confided in a friend that I wanted to be a photojournalist. This was something I had given real thought to. The response that came back to me had something to do with how impossible a field it was to break into and that it was common knowledge that you needed to know someone in the business to even get your foot in the door. Those were scary words. Once again I let it go, and instead I shot weddings and portraits for twenty-something years. It's not that I didn't enjoy that, it's just that I knew in the back of my mind that there were these other things that I had left hanging out there unachieved—possible alternate scenarios that I had been too fearful to create. I had settled and that bothered me. After revisiting those moments I began to get some clarity. For some reason I had decided that it would be wiser to avoid risk rather than risk not succeeding. In retrospect, that was a poor choice. I had let the opinions of others determine what I would do with my life. Of course, I couldn't blame them; the only person responsible for the direction I took my life was me! I couldn't help but feel regret, because I knew my journey would have been a walk in the park compared to what Bobby had to go through to reach her goal.

Of course, my questions then turned to Bobby, and I asked her how she was able to work through that kind of stuff. I knew it had to have come up for her—she must have had her own moments of self-doubt. After all, she went after something that was so far outside of the realm of what was normal for a young woman in those days. I was sure she must have had some underground information on how to handle those moments. I was curious to know what she had discovered that had eluded me. When I asked Bobby how she had done it—how she had put aside so many negative comments, self-doubt, and societal boundaries—her answer was priceless. "I just decided," she said. Then Bobby told me the following story about making decisions:

Bobby on decisions ...

When I was around eleven years of age my mother became ill. At first with diabetes and then not long after that she was diagnosed with severe emphysema caused from years of smoking. Our household was suddenly very focused on getting her well again. With the diabetes, my mother became obsessed with her diet, the foods that we had been used to eating were suddenly cut off and I started to associate food with my mother's illness. I stopped eating. At the time I don't believe there was a name for it, but what I suffered from was anorexia. As my mother's health declined, mine did as well. My father was overwhelmed with concern—first for my mother and then for me. After unsuccessfully trying to address my "eating problem" at home, my father eventually took me to a top psychiatrist in New York. After evaluating the situation, the psychiatrist determined that my mother's failing health was the cause of my condition. He told my father that in order for me to get well I needed be kept away from my mother. At home I lived under the same roof as my mother, but I was isolated from her. It was a sad and lonely time and everything I did suffered because of it—especially my studies.

I had never been a great student. I had always resented that I had to be in a classroom studying mundane subjects instead of with my father learning what I wanted to know, which was to be a doctor. With all that was going on in my life, I really didn't care about my schoolwork and my attitude showed it. As I continued on my downward spiral, my weight continued to drop and I was eventually put into the hospital. Because of that I missed a lot of school and fell even further behind with my schoolwork. During my hospital stay I had a lot of time to think, and I realized my life hand gotten out of hand. I knew I needed to get back to a more normal existence. I woke up one morning and looked at what had become of my body; I knew that what I was doing was damaging, and looking in the mirror I told myself that was enough. I decided I needed to get well and I would do what was necessary to get me there. With that decision made I looked forward to getting home and back to my life, but when I did I saw it was on an altered course. I saw the changes that had taken place in my family and the abrupt end it had brought to my childhood. I knew then there were certain things that I would not be able to change, things that were out of my control, like my mother's illness and the toll it had taken on my family. I realized the only thing that I could control was how I reacted to it, so I began eating again.

When I returned to school I may have been getting physically healthy but I was still miserable. To distract myself from what was going on at home I became a class clown and took to defiant behavior. Of course, that was not very well appreciated by my teachers. One teacher in particular was completely fed up with me. Her name was Miss Plum and though her name may have sounded sweet, she was the complete reverse. Miss Plum was a tall shapeless woman with a cold way about her. She wore her hair in a straight cut and it was as gray as everything else about her. Miss Plum made it clear that she didn't like me, which left me with mutual feelings for her. I remember Miss Plum would roll her eyes or smirk and mumble under her breath when she would overhear me talking to classmates about wanting to become a doctor. It annoyed me, but I never gave her the satisfaction of knowing that.

Due to my lack of interest in school, I was failing several subjects and Miss Plum had no patience with me and would often comment on my poor grades in front of the class. When she left the classroom one day, I stood up in front of the class and did an impersonation of her that was not very flattering. She happened to come back into the classroom in time to catch the end of my act and the resounding round of laughter it had provoked. That infuriated her and she roared angrily in front of the entire class, "Bobby MacGuffie, you will never be a doctor—you will never amount to anything." I never will forget how angry I felt. I was hurt and felt she had no right to say that to me! After that day I was determined to prove her wrong. Her words became my motivation. I went home and begged my parents to get me out of that school. Thankfully, they were able to read the urgency in my voice.

In a matter of days I was sent to live at Miss Beard's boarding school. My parents chose that school because it allowed me to be away from my unsettled home life and it was close enough for me to come home on the weekends and be with my sisters. My first meeting with a teacher at Miss Beard's School was with Miss Henley. When I walked into her classroom she sat me down and said, "So I understand you are interested in science, what kind of research project would you like to work on?"

Since the opportunity to test my new teacher had presented itself, I said, "I would like to do my research on something that involves rats."

To my surprise her answer was, "That will be fine." That was all it took; I was off and running in a new academic direction.

My experience at Miss Beard's school was the complete opposite of Miss Plum's classroom, and I discovered the positive impact of a teacher there. Still, I never lost the desire to prove Miss Plum wrong. I decided that I would do everything within my power to become a doctor. With the decision made, I knew I would need to get serious and start working hard, so I did. During the remainder of my high school years, everything I did was done with a singleness of purpose: to move myself towards the end result that I wanted. With the support of my teachers at Miss Beard's I completely turned myself around and graduated from high school as class valedictorian. When it was time to move on, Miss Beard wanted to be sure she sent me off in the right direction. She did not feel the women's colleges would be a fit for me if my plan was to continue on to medical school. For the first time ever, Miss Beard decided one of her girls should go to a university, despite a student body that would be overwhelmingly male. She felt Cornell was the right school. At the time, I don't think I was aware of how unusual it was for Cornell to accept women. Thanks to Miss Beard and the fact that most of our men were fighting in World War II, Cornell accepted me and I was thrilled.

When I found out I would be going to Cornell, I couldn't wait to go back and see Miss Plum to let her know. When I did, her response was "I hope you are prepared to fail—you don't have a chance of getting through your studies there!"

Seething, I told her, "Miss Plum, not only am I determined not to fail, I fully intend to go on to medical school."

Laughing she said, "Bobby, you will never get accepted into a medical school."

Once again, I left her feeling infuriated! I also left even more determined to succeed. I walked away knowing that failing was not an outcome I would be willing to live with, and I made the decision that I would do everything that I had to do to make sure that didn't happen. So my next goal would be to get through Cornell with the grades that I would need to get me into medical school. With my mind made up—I put my focus where it needed to be and got to work.

the responsibility of responsibility

I **have met many people throughout my life** that are unhappy with what they do for a living and they usually have some explanation for why they are not in the careers that they desire. There is always an excuse in their mind that justifies their reason for being where they are. My excuse was that I had wanted a career that was impossible to get into unless you knew someone. My reality was that I was too fearful of putting my heart into something with the possibility of failing at it. I was afraid of being judged in a negative way so I avoided putting myself in a position where that could happen. What I saw through Bobby's story was that no one is responsible for how things turn out in your life except you and that *you* need to take responsibility for that. By placing blame anywhere else, you will stay stuck in the exact place that you wish to move on from.

Bobby could have easily let Miss Plum's words affect the outcome of her dream to become a doctor. Just like I had let someone's words affect my dreams. Instead, Bobby decided what she wanted, put on her blinders, and did what she needed to make it happen. When I think about how many lives she has positively impacted through her work, it would have been a tragedy if Bobby had let someone else decide her future for her. But Bobby was also lucky because she knew from a young age what she wanted and that never wavered. Most people don't have their life figured out that early or that easily. I was a perfect example of that. I mentioned that to Bobby and asked her if she had any thoughts on how a person could accelerate that process so they don't end up in their forties still wondering what they want to be when they grow up.

Once again I was surprised by the simple constructive answer she offered. Bobby said, "You should always be exploring your interests, trying things out. You should also look for someone who has experience in what you are trying to learn—let them be your guide. Even if what you are exploring doesn't end up being what you want, you will have learned something. Eventually you will know you are on the right track when what you are doing is so rewarding that you are willing to work hard at it without seeing it as a burden."

I found that statement comforting and I allowed myself some slack. I had done that. I had explored my interests—besides shooting weddings and portraits; I also had exhibited and sold some of my photography. Though I enjoyed that, it still missed the mark for me. But working with Bobby, showing her documentary and working with kids through the school assemblies felt different. These things left me with a sense of satisfaction because I felt like I was contributing to something that mattered. Another one of those light-bulb moments occurred! That's what had been missing all these years. I had never gotten that from my work before. Writing this book with Bobby—I was getting it and I felt like I was doing exactly what I was supposed to be doing; and on top of that I seemed to have found my guide.

Strangely, despite my heightened satisfaction, fear struck once again. This time I started worrying that I would do something to screw things up. I started having serious doubts that I would ever be able to clearly get these messages across in book form, never mind get them across well enough that they'd be worthy of readership. Seeing that nothing seemed to push Bobby off course, I figured she might have some insight on how to avoid it myself. Concealing my secret fear, and posing the next question as if it had nothing to do with me, I asked Bobby, "Were you ever worried that you might not see your goal through, and if so, how did you stay on track?"

Bobby answered, "There were things I had to change about myself to see that I accomplished my goals. The first was to make the decision that I would do whatever it took to create the end result that I wanted. There were plenty of times when the distractions of my life could have allowed for a different outcome and there were also times when self-doubt would creep in and I would have thoughts that I had taken on more than I could manage. When that would happen I would push those thoughts out of my mind and tell myself, *I'm going to do it anyway.* Committing to the decision was the first step; once I had that solidified in my mind, I just did what was necessary to follow through, persevere, and make it happen."

Without even realizing it, Bobby had given me just what I needed—a simple anecdote for my biggest problem: self-doubt. More than once I had the thought that I had taken on more than I could handle with this project, and even with how much I wanted it and how good I felt about what I was doing, the fact remained that I had never written a book before. Bobby once again unknowingly moved me with her words. Right then I decided I would just push the negative thoughts aside whenever they would come up. I decided I would do whatever I had to do to get this book written and her story told. I knew it wasn't going to be easy and it would only be accomplished through hard work, but seeing what Bobby had achieved and hearing the stories about what she had to do to get there ... I decided I could do it if I wanted it badly enough, which I did, and I was willing to work hard enough, which I was. I knew there were things that I needed to change about myself to see this project through to the end. I started reading all that I could about writing and I started going to goal-setting workshops and following the advice that these experts offered. I read many books and attended several seminars on the subjects of both writing and goal setting. I made a commitment to telling Bobby's story and I didn't want to let any of my old habits creep back into my life to mess that up. I even called the author of one of the books on writing that I felt was the most helpful to me. He became another guide and helped me through some of the writing issues I faced. I found out that people are willing to help when you are willing to ask. Funnily enough, all the books I was reading about accomplishing goals were telling me the same things that Bobby had figured out on her own. They were offering the same methods that Bobby had used and already shared with me. I decided then that I should believe in the process. I should believe that I could accomplish my goal if I just did whatever I needed to do to make it happen.

Seeing how much Bobby's life was motivating me to go after my dreams, I began to grasp how helpful her story could be in motivating others to go after theirs. This book seemed to have a mind of its own; besides offering a perfect example of what I believed a beautiful and successful person looked like (my original intent), it was turning into a manual for life. As I was writing it I was both getting its messages and putting them out there for future me's. Sure, I would have loved to have gotten these simple pearls of wisdom a few decades sooner, but if I did, I wouldn't have been appreciating them as deeply as I was now, and wouldn't be putting my all into getting the messages out there for others to benefit from. I was exactly where I should have been—in time and place and frame of mind. In this case, having all those years of self-doubt under my belt was actually an advantage. I was able to see firsthand the difference that a positive attitude, hard work, and the unwavering decision to go after a goal could make. With each story Bobby shared, my determination to succeed with this project grew, as did my desire to see to it that the world would get to meet her. The following stories from Bobby about hard work and determination are what kept me going.

Bobby on hard work and tough times ...

Cornell was everything I could have dreamed of. It was a beautiful campus with rolling hills, open land, and city-like buildings. Anything you wanted to know you could find there. There were miles of woods and fields with farming of all kinds. I was completely surrounded by animals, science, and nature. Being in this environment was a wonderful experience. Not only was I living with all of the components that made me happiest, but, I was also physically away from my mother's illness. By this point my mother had developed lung cancer and I hadn't realized how distressed I had been seeing the rapid decline of her health. Being away from that, I could momentarily forget it was happening. I buried myself in my studies and took in the experience with a readiness to learn everything I could. The more involved I got in my classes, the more I knew I was making the right decision in pursuing medicine.

One beautiful spring day I was out enjoying Cornell's campus, hiking with two beagle puppies that I had found and claimed as my own. We were in a secluded area by a gorge that I enjoyed walking along. As I approached a bridge, a tall blonde man came towards me from the other side. The puppies ran towards him and when he bent down to say hello, they were all over him. He seemed to enjoy them as much as they enjoyed him. We struck up a conversation and spent the next two hours walking and talking our way across campus. We discovered we had a lot in common. Both of our fathers were surgeons and we were both in the pre-med program. He talked a lot about his family during that walk and it was obvious they meant a great deal to him. To me they sounded perfect in every way. I was captivated by the stories he shared about his home life and the next thing I knew we were talking on a regular basis and taking frequent walks with the dogs.

Before long Phil and I became a couple and I would often go with him to his parents' home in Utica, New York. They had a beautiful home, complete with Piseco Lake in their backyard. I remember feeling comforted being around Phil's family and I loved spending time with his healthy mother, who very much reminded me of an earlier version of my own mother. Phil's father was a hard working and successful doctor who had a

lively personality and was unaffected by depression and devastation due to a wife's illness. The relationships between his family members left me feeling envious, but at the same time, at ease. The happiness and stability I saw in Phil's family gave me what I lacked in my own. Thinking back, I believe the thing I liked best about Phil was his family.

Initially, I had been hesitant to start any kind of a serious relationship. With all the accelerated pre-med courses I was taking, and the lab work I was doing, I just didn't feel there was room in my life for that, but it happened and it filled a void. When we had been dating for a while, I did bring Phil home to meet my parents. I was reluctant for him to see the stark contrast between our two families but it was unavoidable. I remember how happy my mother was when she met Phil and how much she liked him. She was relieved that her problem child had seemed to settle down and was starting to follow a more typical path. On his first visit, Phil had brought my mother a little silver vase with a rose in it. He had also arranged that she would receive a replacement rose weekly. She was 100 percent for our relationship and I am glad that it was able to bring her some degree of happiness. Phil and I followed the protocol of the day and in a short time we were engaged. My sisters made up small pill capsules with Phil's and my name on it to symbolize our commitment to each other. Funny, but to me I always felt that it better represented my commitment to medicine.

As my relationship with Phil continued I would regularly go home with him and visit his family. On one occasion we had gone to visit his parents at the lake for a weekend. He and I were out for a canoe ride early one morning and I suddenly had an overwhelming urgency to get home. Without any warning I stood up in the canoe and told him I needed to get home. He was confused, and said, "You came to spend the weekend with my family, how can you leave?" I couldn't explain it; I just knew I had to go. I was so frantic about it that I ran from the boat dock back to the house to change into clothing for my trip back home. I packed myself up and Phil took me to the train station. I caught the first train to New York and then a taxi to my home in Passaic, NJ. When I got home that afternoon I ran up the stairs to my mother's bedroom. I got there in time, but my mother passed away a short time after I arrived. It was as though she had waited for me. It was strange but something told me to get there. I am sure I would never have forgiven myself if I had ignored that urge to get home. Since that day I always pay close attention to my instincts.

Not long after my mother died, Phil, like every man of that time, was enlisted in the war effort and sent off to the Pacific in a destroyer. I completely buried myself in my studies. As time went by I started hearing less and less from Phil. Then one day a letter arrived from him and he told me that he had met someone else. In a sense I was relieved. I think my engagement to him was more about the level of normalcy it brought to my life. It was the best thing to happen because with the workload I was taking on, I needed my focus to be on that.

With my engagement to Phil and the death of my mother behind me, I went into such an intense focus on my studies that I don't think

I paid much attention to anything else that was going on—including the fact that my father was in a serious state of depression. Work was my comfort and it completely saved me from all the sadness in my life. I finished school at Cornell in three years and when the time came to move on to medical school, there were many more voices telling me it would be impossible than there were telling me to follow my heart. My desire to be a doctor was the one thing that my father still seemed to take interest in and he was the only one that truly believed in me. He told me, "Bobby, if this is what you want, do not let anyone or anything stand in your way." So I didn't. Even though I was sad to leave Cornell, it was time. I had done well in my pre-med courses and I was finally at the place that I had worked so hard for. I applied to the five medical schools I preferred and, despite the doubt that surrounded me, I was accepted into all five. Since then I never consider another person's negative opinion in regards to what I am capable of.

When I knew I would be going on to medical school, another trip back to see Miss Plum seemed necessary. When I got there she was not in her classroom. I searched the entire school looking for her. I needed her to know that despite her predictions, I had been accepted at all five of the medical schools I had applied to. After a thorough search of the building, I went to the office quite upset. The secretary in the office told me, "Miss Plum is no longer teaching." The news caught me off guard. I was so disappointed; I was filled with the need for her to hear my news. The secretary confided, "Miss Plum had a nervous breakdown, the strain of teaching became too much for her." Leaning closer she whispered to me, "I don't know if you are aware of this, but Miss Plum never wanted to be a teacher; she had always wanted to be a doctor."

I stood there in silence as this new emotion toward Miss Plum washed over me. It was strange, but all I could feel was sadness. I left knowing that I would not need to go back there again. I also left knowing that there really is no need to feel discontent over what another person thinks about you—that displeasure belongs to them. Columbia University's College of Physicians and Surgeons would be the next leg of my journey.

Bobby on more hard work and more tough times ...

Once I got to Columbia, the events of the previous years began to take their toll on me. I was alone in an unfamiliar place and even though I was doing what I had dreamed of since childhood, I felt an overwhelming sadness. I was seeing more of my father because I could go home on weekends, but going home was difficult. It was not the same place. Not only was my mother gone, but essentially my father was gone too. I found myself slipping into depression and I knew I didn't have time for that. I had work to do, and the aftermath of the past few years was making it difficult to function on the level that I needed. I knew I couldn't deal with this on my own and my father was in no condition to help me.

Wanting to be able to focus on what lay ahead of me, I sought out a psychiatrist and handed him my problems. His response was to tell me that I needed to start living a more normal life. He said that I needed to go out and find a man and start living life like a woman. When I left his office that day I felt worse than when I walked in. For as long as I could remember I had been hearing that my life would be easier if I would just conform to what the norm was for my gender. I went home and sat alone in my room mulling over all the moments in my life that I stood apart from what was expected. There seemed to be too many. Taking the advice of the good psychiatrist, I went out and got involved with the first man that paid attention to me. He was also studying to be a doctor at Columbia. Tony was polite and kind and interested in me. He fit the criteria. We started a relationship and within a matter of months I got pregnant. That may not have been normal, but there was no denying that I was certainly living life as a woman. We did what was the only acceptable thing for two people in our situation. Tony and I married and began a hectic life together. When we weren't staying at the hospital, we lived with his mother in her small home in Astoria, New York.

Tony's mother was a wonderful woman and we had a great relationship. She had emigrated from Italy and she really knew how to mother. I sure needed that. When our daughter Chris was born, my mother-in-law was fabulous. She eagerly took on much of the responsibility of caring for the baby. For me, having Chris seemed to be just what I needed. I loved her so much and she totally did away with any feelings of depression I had been having.

Tony and I were incredibly busy with school and our training and we were spending a good deal of our time on different schedules. I would stay at the hospital every other night and be at home with Chris on the alternate nights. We would sometimes go three weeks without getting to spend a day together.

Besides school, Tony had the added pressure of being in the service. When Chris was around two years old, Tony was sent to Colorado for basic training. While he was gone I kept at my chaotic schedule. Between residency and caring for a baby, it was a demanding time. But I was totally engrossed with my work and loving it, and then to top it off, I would go home to a beautiful baby that I completely adored.

A rare day off with
Tony and Chris

Around the same time that Tony and I married, my father remarried. She was a nurse that he had worked with for a number of years and my sisters and I hoped this would help bring back the man my father had once been. Although he did seem to rally slightly, it didn't last. He was a different man from the father I had adored and idolized as a child. It was difficult to see and I missed the man he was.

With his training for the Air Corps, Tony would be away for long stretches of time. When he could get home, we tried to resume a normal married life, but it was difficult. We were living completely separate lives. We hardly ever saw each other when we were in the same state and living under the same roof. With Tony being on the other side of the country, it left very little chance of constructing a marriage. Though Tony was in the service—he was not in combat and was never sent overseas—Tony was more or less living a college existence and his leisure time while he was away was not being spent as a married man. He was free of the daily responsibility and was not feeling the need to stay loyal to a family that was so far away. During one of his trips home on leave, I did manage to get pregnant again. I worked throughout my pregnancy, while my mother-in-law watched Chris, and Tony came home once in a while. It was not a normal marriage and it was starting to become obvious that making our marriage work seemed too difficult and might not have been a priority for either of us.

With a three-year-old daughter, a new pregnancy, and a husband who was away both physically and emotionally, plus the last leg of medical school on the horizon, it was a crazy time. A time so busy that it barely allowed for sleep. On top of everything that was already a priority, I found myself with a new one. Chris had developed a serious skin condition that required hospitalization. It turned into a life-threatening situation because it had become infected and the infection had gotten into her bloodstream. I never experienced worry at this level before. This was my child and I could lose her. I never left the hospital. I spoke with everyone I could about her condition. I was in the medical field and my child was seriously ill; that did not sit well with me. I became acutely aware of what my father must have felt during the course of my mother's illness and eventual death. It is what placed him in the deep depression that he could not seem to break free from. He had never gotten over my mother suffering so much in her last years, and that as a physician he was unable to do anything to stop it. Seeing Chris so sick gave me a clear understanding of my father's emotional state and I began to feel a strong need to take some action on his behalf. I worried about his inability to break out of his depression. It concerned me enough that I scheduled an appointment with the top psychiatrist at Columbia. It was a Saturday and I was at the hospital with Chris; I called my father to tell him I had made an appointment for him to meet with a doctor who could help him. The appointment was set for Monday morning. I told my father I would bring him in for the appointment, and if he wanted, I would stay with him throughout the meeting. During the same phone call, I made arrangements with my stepmother to come to the hospital to see Chris. Sunny, my new stepmother was an exceptional nurse and had a great track record as a diagnostician. She and I set up a time to meet the next day to evaluate Chris's progress.

On Sunday, Chris's condition started improving. I met up with Sunny at the hospital and after seeing that Chris was doing better we were both glad she had some good news to bring home to my father. I told Sunny that getting the psychiatrist to treat my father would bring more good news. She and I were upbeat and excited about the new direction in which things were going. About two hours after I put my stepmother in a taxi heading back home to my father, I received a phone call from her. "He's dead!" her voice screamed into the phone. As the newspaper described, "Dr. Robert MacGuffie took his own life with his old army pistol which was found at his side."

Losing my father by his own hand left me devastated. I felt guilty because I believed I should have acted sooner on his behalf. I was overwhelmed by what he had done and saddened to think that it was the only way he thought he could stop the pain he was in. My answer to the pain and loss that I felt was to once again bury myself in my work. Being in a field where my function was to help ease other people's pain seemed to make it easier to avoid the unpleasant task of focusing on my own.

keep moving forward

T**here is nothing I could compare** in my own life experiences that could come close to the difficulties that Bobby had to endure while working toward her goal. Looking at my own decision to give up on my dreams based on the comments of a few people seemed ridiculous after hearing what Bobby had to deal with. It was an important lesson not only for me, but also for the kids we were going out and speaking to. The work we were doing with the kids through the school programs became even more important to me. I felt compelled to get this point across to them. Even though I believed in what we were saying to these kids, my own familiar habit of self-doubt was hard to break, and added to that issue, I had a new one. That being age—which was no longer creeping up on me, but was galloping up on me. I couldn't help but wonder if being in my late forties made it a bit too late to be heading off toward the dreams of my past. Of course, working alongside Bobby delivering the messages of belief in oneself, perseverance, and hard work would not allow for me to continue with those thoughts. Through Bobby's story I had learned that self-doubt was detrimental to success, and that perseverance was the number one weapon to choose when battling it. The secret is to keep moving forward. So during the moments when my head was filled with the uncertainty I had towards my ability to head off in a brand new direction and get a book written and published at the point that I was in life, I kept the lessons I was learning from Bobby at the forefront. Work hard, push unhelpful thoughts aside, and never give up. Bobby's struggles once again offered useful lessons. This time in perseverance:

Bobby on perseverance ...

For seven years I bounced around filling positions that needed to be filled, learning new things all along the way. I did my internships and residencies in general medicine, neurosurgery, orthopedic surgery, general surgery, cancer surgery, as well as reconstructive work. Though I enjoyed them all, the time had come for me to make a decision as to which direction I would go with my training. I knew I wanted to be a surgeon, and since I preferred putting things back together rather than taking things apart, I felt plastic surgery was a good choice for me. It was a fairly new field and it just so happened that one of the founders and chairman of the American Board of Plastic Surgery, Dr. Jerome Webster, was at Columbia and about to take on his last resident for training in his field of specialty. I wanted that position. Everyone at the hospital told me to forget about it—my peers as well as some of the top doctors I had already trained with. It was a much sought after spot and Dr. Webster had never trained a woman. He had also made it clear that he had no intention of ever doing so. During that time, I didn't care much about what anybody else thought. I wanted that position and I let it be known.

For the age I was and the accomplished people I was working with, it may seem strange that I wasn't intimidated. I'm pretty sure my attitude stemmed from what I had already been through; after that, there wasn't much to be afraid of. That worked in my favor.

While I was doing my residency, my time was spent mainly in the operating room. Each year the responsibility became heavier. It was like climbing a pyramid. As the time went on there were fewer people to compete with, but that also meant less people to do the work. Being the only woman that was in the running for surgical residency was not making me a particular favorite among the male residents.

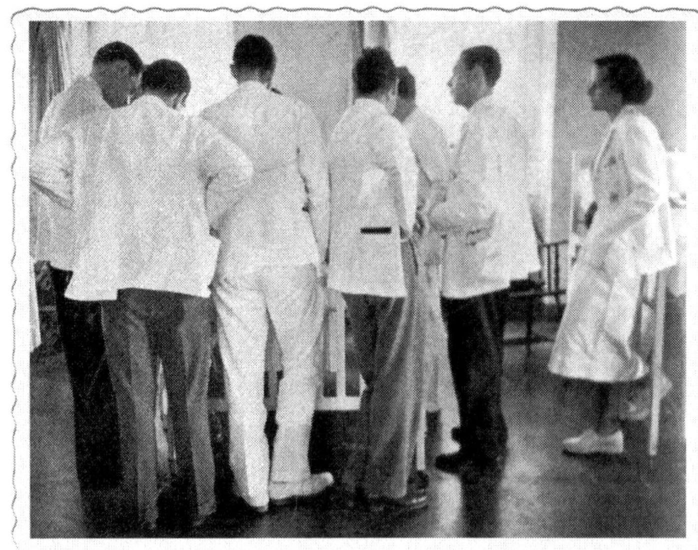

Ed Feingersh/Getty Images

It certainly didn't help when McCall's magazine called and asked to do a story about me. The article was to be titled "The Doctor is a Mother." It was all about how unusual I was for that time—a woman doctor with a family, and then on top of that being a surgeon. On the day I was approached about the magazine article I was told by the head of the hospital that I needed to attend a special luncheon to discuss the details and that I should come looking my best. The meeting would introduce me to the head of McCall's magazine, the editor, the writer, and the photographer that would shoot the spread. I was not at all keen on the idea. I was incredibly busy with work and the thought of having a photographer shadow me for several weeks would be a huge inconvenience. I was twenty-five years old, had just gone through six grueling years of residency, hardly ever slept and was only getting home to see my child every other night. On those nights at home I had to squeeze in as much time with Chris and Tony as I could. I was very protective of my limited amount of free time and I did not want to give any of it away to a magazine story. But the hospital wanted me to do it, so I was told to attend the luncheon to hear what I was in for. I was reminded again to come looking my best.

In an effort to please the hospital administration, I arrived dressed in a crisp white uniform with my hair more attended to than it normally would have been. When I sat down at the table, I was introduced to the men I would be working with. The head of McCall's took one look at me and said, "Are you sure she's only twenty-five, she looks a lot older than that." That was all I needed. I didn't want to be there to begin with.

I stood up and said, "Good. That lets me out of it." I also added, "I think you should go get yourself the youngest most beautiful model you can find and have her come and live my life for a month—then take her picture and see what she looks like." I was glad to be done with the whole thing and I got up and started to walk away. The next thing I knew the head of the hospital was escorting me back to the table.

He spoke into my ear and as we walked back to the group of men I had walked away from, he informed me, "This article is not about you, it is about what is good for the hospital." He said, "And don't forget—what is good for the hospital is also what is good for you." I sat back down and listened to what the next several weeks of my life would be like.

As it turned out, the article, and particularly the photographs, really told the story of what my life was like back then. Not long after the story ran, which was not long after my father's death, my marriage to Tony came to an end.

Despite being pregnant with our second child we just could not make it work. I had already dealt with losing my mother and my father. Now it was my husband. It was just another stress added to an already full plate. In our four years of marriage, Tony and I rarely saw each other so it was not so much losing our relationship that was difficult. It was the starting over and getting resettled with Chris along with the addition of a new baby. I did what I had to, moved forward, and started the next phase of my life. Single with one child and another on the way, I moved into a one-room apartment on New York's Riverside Drive. I contacted my

Ed Feingersh/Getty Images

childhood caretaker, Re-Re, and she moved in and cared for Chris. Then I got back to work—pregnant and focused on doing what I needed to do to get the surgical internship I wanted. My father had always told me that I could achieve whatever I wanted as long as I wanted it badly enough and was willing to work hard at it. I held onto those words and refused to let the fear of rejection or my personal issues stop me from going after what I wanted.

After my second daughter, Martha, was born I continued to take Chris and the new baby back to Astoria to see my mother-in-law. Despite my separation from Tony, his mother had always been wonderful with Chris and I felt it was important for her to know Martha too. On one such visit the girls and I had spent what I thought was a lovely afternoon with Tony's mom. When it came time to leave she started getting emotional. She began crying about how the changes that had taken place between Tony and I had also affected her life. She missed being a part of her grandchildren's everyday life. I started getting uncomfortable with the direction in which things were going. I gathered the kids and their belongings and went outside to wait for a taxi back to Riverside Drive. My mother-in-law followed me out to the street and a fight ensued between mother and grandmother. She grabbed my baby out of my arms and would not give her back to me. I had Chris in my other arm and whatever paraphernalia that comes with two small children. I was alone and had never been in a situation where someone was physically trying to take from me what was rightfully mine. It must have been quite a sight for the neighbors.

Somehow my mother-in-law managed to get Martha into her house and locked me out. The police came but were unable to confirm that the baby belonged with me. It was terrible; I ended up having to go to court before I was able to get Martha back from her. It was a fight well fought on both parts—neither of us willing to part with Martha. But she was my baby, and as much as I liked my mother-in-law, I was not about to sacrifice my child for her. That pretty much put an end to the friendly relationship I had enjoyed with her.

Back at the hospital the time had come for me to commit to my specialty and I was still waiting to hear if I would get the plastic surgery residency. During my rounds one day I was in the room of a young patient. Tests had just confirmed that the boy was suffering from an aggressive form of cancer and that it was terminal. As I delivered this news to the boy's father, the man passed out and struck his head on a radiator that he was standing near. He received a substantial gash on his head that required immediate attention. I got a gurney, and with the help of a few residents got him on it and wheeled him to the emergency room. I repaired his head wound and returned him to his son's room. Although it was against hospital regulations, I also arranged to have a bed put in the boy's room so his father could stay with him. The next day I was called down to Dr. Webster's office. He told me that he had a look at the repair I had done on the man's head and that he was quite impressed since he hadn't yet had the opportunity to train me. It turned out that the man whose head I had stitched was Dr. Webster's best friend. Dr. Webster told me he was very grateful for what I had done for his friend and how I had handled the situation. He also informed me he was willing to take me on as his last resident. He said, "I can see that you are serious about your career, and since you already have a husband and two children and are settled with your family life, I will take you on as my last trainee."

I was thrilled to know that my dedication had convinced him to go against his better judgment and take a chance on training a woman. I was also relieved to know that he knew nothing about my life on Riverside Drive where my two children were without a father and I was without a husband. It was probably also good that he hadn't heard anything about my recent street fight and court case.

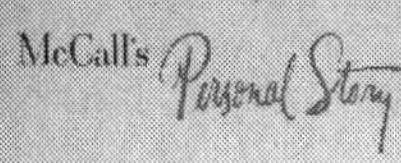

the doctor is a mother

A woman who wants to be a doctor must give up most of the things she loves—including some of the best years of her life. But it can be worth it

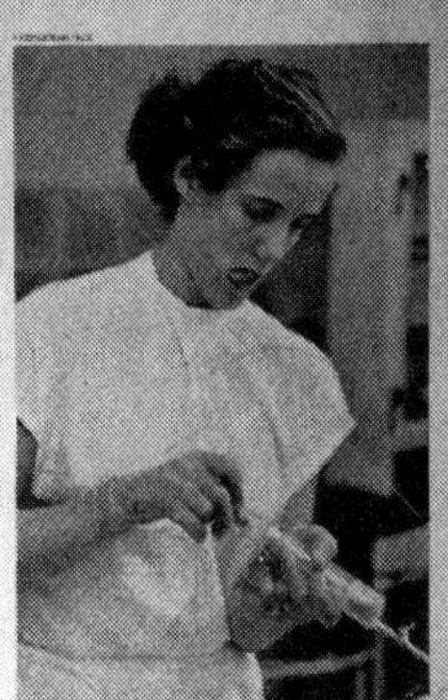

Removing fluid from a patient's chest is only one of ticklish jobs an intern must do. Martha is responsible ... wards, is on call at all hours for emergencies like this, which she must be able to size up and handle herself

MARTHA MORGAN MACGUFFIE has been studying to be a doctor since she was 7, when she used to make hospital rounds with her surgeon father in Passaic, New Jersey. At 8 she was reading medical books, mostly on obstetrics. At 9 she was photographed in a doctor's smock, armed with a carving knife. At Columbia's College of Physicians and Surgeons she married Tony, another medical student. Now 25, Martha has been at New York City's Presbyterian Hospital two years. Tony is a resident physician at Montefiore Hospital.

Only a girl dedicated to medicine could survive the life Martha leads. She gets up at 6:00 to start a working day which may last 18, 24 or even 36 hours. An average night's sleep is 5 hours. She and Tony are home together only every other evening. Their combined annual hospital pay is $600. With this, and a small sum left Martha by her father, they just get by. They can't yet spend as much time as they'd like with their daughter Chris, 3, but fortunately there's a mother-in-law "who's a lamb."

"Of course we don't like being separated like this," Martha admits. "But this way, being together is a treat for us both." At home Martha insists on being "Mrs.," not "Dr." For, she says, "My whole life there is my husband and baby. Tony's the boss."

Life at Presbyterian is tense, but it has its tender moments too. "Why, you know," she says, "if I ever lose a patient, I feel like going off in a corner and having a good cry."

It's late at night, but the day that's ended has merged into the day that's already begun. And still there's work to do. Dr. MacGuffie has been on duty since 7:00 a.m. Now, exhausted, she's catching a nap on a stretcher, awaiting her next emergency case

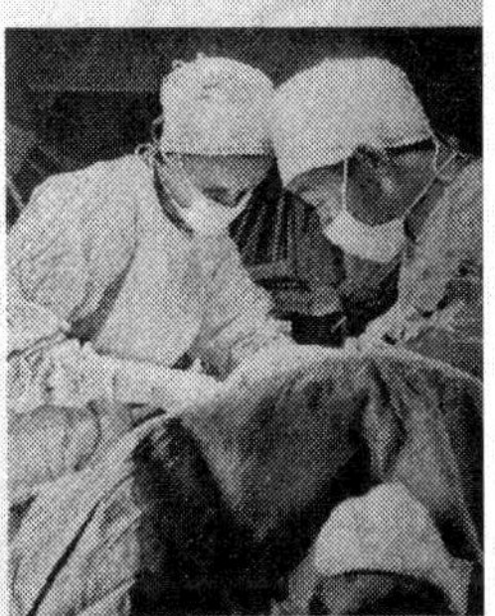

Martha averages two to four operations a day. They begin at 8:00 in the morning and take from two to nine hours. Martha assists the surgeon on difficult cases, but "under supervision we interns handle the simpler ones ourselves"

Ed Feingersh/Getty Images

lesson learned

A**fter hearing about this time** in Bobby's life, I decided that adversity was something that could either cripple you or show the world what you are made of. I remember a wedding that I photographed many years ago. The father of the bride had recently lost his leg below the knee to diabetes. When it came time to take the family photographs he refused to participate. He didn't want to be photographed without his leg. No matter how much his wife or daughter begged him to join the rest of the family, he turned them down and sat in the corner of the room wallowing in self-pity. I felt bad for his family because of the pain it put them through in that moment. I also felt sad for him for letting something that was out of his control take away from a moment of happiness that was within his control.

About ten years after that wedding, my own mother lost her leg at the hip to cancer. A few days after her surgery she was racing my seven-year-old son down the hospital corridor with her walker. She wanted to make sure he knew she was still the same old Nana. Unlike the man at the wedding, my mother and Bobby decided it best to show the world what they are made of. Thankfully, I have not had to deal with anything as difficult as either of them, and hope I never have to. But if I do face a serious challenge, I hope I model myself after them. Actually, it would be a good idea to model myself after them even without the adversity. I figure if my mother can still do things like cook meals for twenty-five of us, or maintain her hillside garden, or wallpaper her kitchen, or race her grandson down a hospital hallway with one leg, and if Bobby was able to get through the grueling workload of medical school and residencies while burying two parents and raising two children alone, not to mention what was yet to come for her, I should be able to accomplish a few of the things that I want to get done.

We all have our own set of circumstances that shape our lives. Some of them are good and some are not. What I have finally learned is that the end product comes down to your reaction to the circumstance. A lot of the time we hold on to a belief from an experience we had in the past and it becomes something we live by. When we allow that to happen we are allowing that to dictate our reactions to future circumstances. For me, I believed I could never become a photojournalist or a writer because it was just too hard. I just didn't believe that I had what it took. By not believing, I created that exact outcome. Bobby created her own outcome too. Hers ended the way she had planned. That happened because she decided what she wanted, set goals, did what was needed to see them through, and persevered despite numerous obstacles.

What I picked up from Bobby was that if you want to succeed at something you have to believe in yourself. If you don't believe in yourself you have to learn how to push those thoughts out of your head and change them into thoughts that are useful. It doesn't matter what we determine the reason is for not going after what we want in life. For some people it is the fear of failure, for others it is blame placed on unsupportive parents or spouses, or for others it may be financial issues or tragic events that may have occurred in their lives. No matter what it is, it all comes down to one thing. There is not another soul in this world that is responsible for the direction that your life goes but you.

I read somewhere that lack of self-confidence is one of the biggest problems facing individuals in every culture. It is sad that people can be so filled with self-doubt that they are willing to go through life compromising and settling for something less than what they really want, but it happens all the time. On this subject I speak from experience. Whether it was sheer coincidence or a series of events that were meant to happen in my life to bring me to Bobby's door and teach me this, I finally got it.

After seeing what Bobby accomplished in Kenya in her sixties, seventies, and eighties, she also taught me that you are never too old to go after what you want in life. There is no finish line. Life is for living, loving, and learning till that very last day. So with each wall I smack into, I will keep moving forward with my focus on what I need to do to get around any obstacle that tries to get in my way. I now know that efforts are worthwhile, no matter what age a person is when they set out to accomplish them.

As Bobby and I have been traveling to schools and speaking to kids about the three principles that have shaped Bobby's life, the kids have asked some very essential questions. I feel it is important to hear what those questions are and also share what Bobby—with her eighty-five years of experience—has offered in response. Maybe you will find the answers to your own questions here.

The Pepis Studio

Symptom:

I am not sure what I want to be or
what I want to do with my life.
How will I know if I am on the right path?

Name Date

Address

Rx

Always be exploring your interests.
You will know when you have found the thing you were meant to do when you are willing to work hard at it without it feeling like a burden.

Signature *Martha M. MacGuffie, MD*

Symptom:

I know what I want to do—
but I think it is going to be too difficult.
I don't know if I will be able to succeed.
What should I do?

Name ———————— *Date* ————

Address ————————————

Rx

Push any negative thoughts out of your mind and focus on what you need to do to succeed at your goal.

Signature **Martha M. MacGuffie, MD**

Symptom:

I have tried before to achieve my goal
but I have failed.
Does that mean I chose the wrong goal?

Name ——————————— *Date* ————

Address ———————————————

Rx

Failures are meant to teach us
something. Learn from them and
commit to staying on course.
Then do what is necessarry to
achieve your goal.

Signature Martha M. MacGuffie, MD

lesson two

Look for
the
Silver
Lining
Lynn Cluess Manzione

turn it around

"Even in the most difficult situations, you can turn it around and find something good in it."
—Dr. Robert N. MacGuffie

Once again the quote that introduces this lesson was offered to Bobby as a child from her father. Without sounding too cliché, all of the little messages he handed over to Bobby seemed to become words to live by. This particular one I could definitely relate to. Strangely enough, I seemed to be in the middle of experiencing it. If I hadn't had my accident, broken my jaw in three places, dislocated it, damaged nine of my teeth and spent a year recovering from it all, I never would have met Bobby and ended up on this incredible journey. If I had not had that accident I would not have taken the chance at writing. If it were not for Bobby and her story I would not have had the opportunity to be a part of getting these important messages out to the kids we were reaching through the school programs we were doing. If it weren't for that accident and meeting Bobby I would never have known how important that was to me. It was important because if I could, I wanted to help prevent others from ending up middle-aged before they figured out what they wanted in life—feeling guilty for wasted time. Without the accident that led me to Bobby I would still be in that place. I know it sounds crazy but I do believe that Bobby and I met for a reason, and as unpleasant an experience Bobby had in the upcoming story, I believe her pain and loss happened for a reason too. Obviously, Bobby would have preferred not to have experienced the tragedy of losing her sons, but she is very aware that if that hadn't occurred, she would never have ended up touching the lives of thousands of orphans in Africa.

Children have always been a big part of Bobby's life. She has healed many, she has helped many, and she has had many. She has also lost three too many, and that is a load that seems impossible to carry. How she helped herself get through that dark period shows once more that Bobby believed in her father's words. If I didn't know the timeline, I would have suspected that Bobby's father came upon this belief after seeing what his daughter was able to do with her grief.

Bobby on good times and bad and making the best of them all ...

Just when things seemed to settle, and I was getting used to my life without Tony, along came Dr. Perry Hudson. He was lured to Columbia from Johns Hopkins as a Damon Runyon Cancer Fellow and was given a large research department at the hospital. He was also given the position of Professor of Urology. My first introduction to him was through a patient I treated. It turned out that this particular patient was supposed to be joining Dr. Hudson as his head researcher.

When I met my new patient, he was on the psych ward. As I entered his room I found him to be despondent; I also found his wife to be badgering him relentlessly. Seeing what condition the man was in, I ordered his wife to be removed from his room and I put my assessment on the man's chart. "Patient seems to have suffered an emotional breakdown. I believe his wife to be at the root of his problem." When Dr. Hudson entered the room and looked at his employee's chart, he was quite displeased with my diagnosis. His reaction was, "Great, a woman doctor!" After Dr. Hudson met the wife that I believed to be at the root of the problem, it didn't take him long to change his view of my assessment.

Dr. Hudson and I were introduced a second time, by my senior attending physician, Dr. Cushman Haagensen. Dr. Haagensen was a world-famous authority on breast cancer and I had the good fortune to become his chief resident in surgery. Dr. Haagensen thought very highly of me and we had become good friends. He also knew about my situation with the recent coming apart of my marriage and had an inkling that Dr. Hudson and I had a lot in common. Dr. Hudson's marriage had also recently ended. Introductions were made. Instincts were correct. Perry and I quickly became inseparable. Our courtship seemed to last all of about fifteen minutes! As soon as all divorces were final, we married and adoptions took place. Perry had four children from his first marriage, and when his youngest daughter Harriet met me, she decided that she was going to stay with us. So Perry with Harriet, and I with Chris and Martha, all moved in together and became a rather large instant family. Well, we thought we were a large family—until we added five more kids to the count and found out what large was.

The fifteen years between 1948 and 1963 seemed to find me consistently pregnant. The result was eight children. It was also during those years that I completed medical school, did my residencies, started performing surgeries, opened my private practice and had a research lab in my home. In our lab we were studying the effects of cigarette smoke for the tobacco industry. Based on our findings I was asked to testify in Washington, D.C., before the Senate. Due to what seemed to be a chronic condition, I arrived eight months pregnant to do so.

Another very important position held during those years was that of Girl Scout troop leader. I am positive I was not the typical scout leader because I showed the girls what I knew, which was science. I'm not sure how much my troop of girls enjoyed going to Helen Hayes Rehabilitation Hospital to learn about quadriplegic boys who were in their situation as a result of poor choices. I'm also not sure it was the most Girl Scout-like experience when I took them to a pathology lab where they were presented a freshly prepared brain of a seventeen-year-old that had played chicken with a car on one of our local roadways! These may not have been typical scouting experiences but they were definitely learning experiences.

Those years of young children were considerable, and, of course, I found myself having two full time jobs: mother and doctor. When I think about having eight children I am still not sure how that happened while so much else was going on. It wasn't exactly a plan; it just occurred and we were happy for it. So many times people have asked me how I did it, combining the two. I can only say that I seemed to know what the best choice was for a particular situation in that moment. I also must give credit to the resiliency of children. Except for an occasional objection from one of the youngest of the brood, who on rare occasions would say, "Please don't leave me," I did my best to choose what I thought was the most important thing at the time. Which was either to appease one of the children or to leave them for a pressing medical situation, which at that moment was obviously my responsibility. Looking back, I can't comprehend how I made it through those years. What I do know is that I wouldn't have made it if it weren't for the wonderful women that helped me raise my children. There were three of them that saw us through those incredibly hectic years and I know I could never thank them enough for the love and care that they gave to us all.

The years that came after Perry and I transitioned from our first marriages to our marriage to each other were wonderful years. We were busy with our work but we loved the time we had together; both of us having left marriages that felt empty at the end, were truly happy together and really appreciated each other. Aside from the financial struggle that came with raising eight children, it was an exceptionally happy time of life. The kids all seemed content and easily adjusted to the changes. Being that we had so many kids and they all had someone close in age, they never lacked playmates. The five girls were the oldest—Harriet, Chris, Martha, Janey, and Pam—and then we finally had a boy. Scott was born eleven months after Pam and the two of them were inseparable in their early years. All of the children shared my love for animals, so aside from our home being filled with kids, it was also filled with four-legged creatures. From children to raccoons to ferrets to retired racehorses, our home was always filled with life, and to this day—even though the kids are gone—I have never been without an animal in my home.

Harriet
Chris
Martha
Scott
Pam
Janey
Rob
Reid

In the late 1950s Perry was running the research lab out of our home in Palisades, New York. He had moved it into the house after he had a falling out at Columbia. He took his grant and some of his best researchers and we made room for them in our home. It was obviously not the ideal situation, and as our family was growing, it was becoming more difficult. One Saturday afternoon Perry received a phone call from a friend, he left saying he was not sure when he would return. When he arrived later that afternoon he told me not to make any plans for the next day, he had somewhere he wanted to take me. That was all he would say about it.

The next morning we got in the car and went for a ride. About twenty minutes later we turned off a winding country road, up a long driveway and parked the car in front of a sizeable stone house. Perry turned to me and said, "So how do you like your new home?" It was like nothing I had ever seen before. A magnificent replica of a Scottish manor house with the look and feel of a castle, it immediately felt like home and I knew it was going to be an ideal place to raise our family. It was unfortunate that the ability to pay for the house had come from an inheritance after Perry's parents passed away, but it was wonderful that we would be able to have a place in which we could all fit. The house had been unoccupied for a year prior to our arrival—which meant we had some cleaning up to do. Part of that meant getting the squirrels that had been squatting there to move out and find a place of their own. Surprisingly, no exterminators were necessary … we had six kids … the squirrels willingly moved on.

We moved into our new home two days before Christmas and it quickly became ours. It had eight bedrooms and five bathrooms and we used them all. Having been used to living in much tighter quarters, and with their sights set on finding their own personal space, the kids scrambled to pick out bedrooms. If things were good before, they were great now. Work and home were separate and the kids were having a great time exploring their new surroundings. Aside from the house, which was perfect, there were thirty-two acres of land complete with a stable, which we filled with horses. We had a tennis court and a pool and when we weren't working, we did lots of entertaining. Life really could not have been better!

Not long after we moved into our new home, we also had another

son. Robbie made number seven. During my pregnancy with Rob, I had been fearful that something was wrong. Having been through so many pregnancies I knew this one was different. I became rather depressed about it and it would upset Perry when I spoke about feeling that way. After Rob was born, and everything appeared to be fine, Perry voiced his unhappiness that I had put us both through so much. At the time I couldn't help it; it seemed to me that the activity during my pregnancy with Rob started so much sooner than any of the others, and that the movement was tenfold that of what I had experienced with any of my other pregnancies. It wasn't long after Rob was born before I was pregnant again and for the second time started feeling those same symptoms. This time I was not as concerned because everything with Rob had seemed to turn out fine.

When Rob was just about two years old the fearful thoughts that I had during his pregnancy were confirmed. I went into his bedroom one morning to get him dressed and found Rob's trunk and extremities covered with hemorrhages. I immediately called our pediatrician and he told us to bring him to the local hospital right away. It was a Saturday morning and they did a rapid series of blood tests in the emergency room. What they found was a marked abnormality when they screened his blood for platelets, the lack of which had caused the hemorrhagic condition.

We immediately made arrangements to take Rob to Johns Hopkins hospital to be seen by the head of the pediatric hematology department. While we waited for the results of all of the testing that had to be done, he was started on cortisone. The response to the medications was poor.

He was admitted to the hospital and eventually the cause of the blood abnormality was diagnosed. It was a very rare condition of the bone marrow called Fanconi's Anemia. Rob's medications were increased and the obvious bleeding areas went away. The disease was characterized by interference with bone growth, a severe bleeding tendency and hyper-reflexivity (very fast reflexes). That explained the constant movement I had felt during his pregnancy. At a time when everything in our lives had been working out beautifully, this cast such darkness over our family. From that day forward Rob's life was complicated and disrupted by the side effects of both drugs and hormone changes. In the meantime I gave birth to our youngest boy, Reid, and I waited for the ax to fall.

Reid was a small baby when he was born. He was beautiful and much quieter than the others were as babies. He stayed that way and his speech did not seem to develop in the same time frame as his older siblings. At age two he developed the same symptoms as his brother Rob and then we had two sick children to worry over and run to doctors with.

Some of the characteristics of Fanconi's were that the boys' growth was stunted and they had absent opponent muscles in their thumbs. For Reid he also was missing inner ear bones in both ears. That explained his delayed speech and quiet ways. Rob had a missing genitourinary system (GU tract) but he never had trouble from it. Despite the missing muscles in their thumbs, which left them with limited hand movement, they both adjusted and did quite well. Rob was a very talented musician and took to the guitar. His disability never got in the way of his playing and he became an incredible guitarist.

Although Reid had a hearing loss, which caused some speech problems, he preferred not having his hearing aids in. This caused a problem for him one day when at about age five he wandered away from some of his older sisters while they took him on a hike at High Tor, a state park near our home that has trails leading to the top of the mountain.

When they realized he was no longer nearby, they frantically started calling for him. Reid was nowhere to be found and eventually the search included the local police and park rangers. We were all getting frantic, it was early October but it could get quite cold on the mountain once the sun went down. We had a large search party going over every inch of the state park. They covered all the trails along the mountainside. Hours had passed and it had gotten dark. It was a confusing scene and there were people all over our property. Needless to say we were thrilled when Reid emerged from the woods at the edge of our property, walked up to one of the people involved in the search and said, "What the hell is going on around here?" His version of the story was that the other guys got lost. After an emotional reunion I sent him into the bath to get cleaned up. I wanted to take him down to the firehouse where the search team was waiting. I felt he should thank them for the time they had spent looking for him. While Reid was in the bath, the chief of police came to the house. After he and I spoke, the Chief walked into the bathroom where Reid was in the tub.

"Well young man," he said, "you are lucky to have made it back." The Chief lectured a while longer while Reid sat quietly in the bath. After he

had gotten his point across, he left.

When Reid finished up with his bath he came out and with an indignant look on his face said, "That guy has a hell of a nerve coming into the bathroom while I was naked!" Reid may not have been a big talker, but when he did, he kept us laughing.

A decision we had to make early on for the boys was how we would deal with their childhood. We had to weigh the dangers of what they wanted to do against how it could affect their health. Being that Fanconi's Anemia is a blood disorder and is characterized by lack of platelets, doing anything that could bring on bleeding posed serious consequences for them. We already knew that their diagnosis could be grave even though they had a milder case than others with the disease. One of the symptoms of the disease is hyper-reflexivity; for them that meant amazing speed and unbelievable coordination and body control. They were always the fastest kids in their age groups. They could also stop and change direction in a way that was extremely unusual. This gave them excellent athletic abilities. For Rob, who loved football, it meant he was one of the best players on any field he would play on. That of course, made him love the game even more. While Rob's passion was football, Reid developed a love for speed. He became an avid go-cart racer. Perry bought him his first go-cart and we just held our breath hoping for good driving skills. Thankfully, that was something Reid possessed. Again, it was a symptom of Fanconi's disease that allowed him to excel at his sport of racing. He had extremely quick reactions and was able to out-maneuver his opponents with ease.

As the boys became more involved with their sports, we were faced with the decision of whether or not they should be allowed to participate in the things they obviously loved. It was a decision that I discussed in depth with their pediatric hematologist. The end result of those conversations was to let them live as normal a life as possible and hope for the best, so that's what we did. I lived in constant fear that one of them would get hurt, but I knew it was important for them to experience some joy to counter all the unpleasantness that came with their disease. Though it was never discussed with them, both Rob and Reid seemed to know that their disease could turn out badly. Because of that I feel like they squeezed as much enjoyment and living into their days as possible.

Rob's personality was fairly sunny and he was quite gregarious. Even though he was much shorter than his teammates on the football team, he seemed to always be the one surrounded by the girls. The other players would watch him from across the field with their mouths hanging open. I'm sure it baffled them that this little guy with the unusual looks was getting all of the girls' attention. The reason was that Rob was a good listener and a caring friend. He loved people and instinctively knew how to make them feel good about themselves.

Reid was more of a loner. Having a hearing loss probably added to that. He had a vivid imagination, though, and was a very creative child. When he was really little, I was fascinated with his mind's eye. He seemed to live in a fantasy world a good deal of the time. Reid also loved animals of any kind. He often took to adopting chipmunks (chip monkeys as my daughter Janey used to call them) or baby raccoons. He would vehemently defend them when he would come in bitten by one or another. "It was my fault," he would say. "I must have annoyed them." Reid had a way about him that just made you smile.

Reid's personality differed from Rob's in that he could fly into rages quite unexpectedly. That was the result of the heavy doses of steroids he was on. Where Rob for the most part took it in stride when he needed to go into the hospital or get his transfusions, Reid would go into battle mode. One particular time this occurred while I was driving home from a doctor's appointment with Reid and we had just found out that he would need to have another transfusion. When we got into the car, he was so angered by the news that he went into a full rage. He swung his arms at me and hit me in the throat while I was driving. The steroids they were on produced abnormal strength in the boys and when he did this I was struggling to breath from the impact. I remember telling him I would need to pull off the highway and stop at the hospital so they could check me. Knowing how severe his rages could get, my real intention was to get help in calming him down. When we got to the hospital they took him to a room and it took seven nurses to restrain him. He still broke free and tried to jump out a window before a large orderly was able to wrestle him to the ground.

Those rages were frightening. Another one came while at home one day. Again, I had just told him that he was going to have to go back to the hospital for another blood transfusion. He grabbed an ax from an antique suit of armor that decorates a corner of our living room. He chased me all along the quiet mountain road that we live on. Thankfully, I had gotten a head start. I was able to make it to a neighbor's house before he caught up with me. It got fairly crazy dealing with the side effects of their disease and it brought another element of difficulty to our home life. But when Reid wasn't dealing with the effects of the steroids, he was a happy, pleasant child who kept us entertained; it was just difficult not knowing when one of these outbursts could occur.

Through the years, the boys spent a large amount of time in hospitals and doctors' offices undergoing tests and treatments. Their disease was rare and not well studied so they were of great interest to the medical field. We felt it was important for researchers to learn as much about the disease as possible so we spent many hours taking them back and forth to Children's Hospital in Boston where the research team was based. It was an incredibly stressful time and it affected everyone in the family. When you have a sick child, it overshadows everyone else's life. When you have two sick children, it takes away so much from the other children. No matter how aware you are of their suffering, there is not much that can be done to change it. The pain and difficulty it brought into the lives of all of my children, and that I could do nothing to alleviate it, is one of my biggest heartaches.

It seemed so unfair for everyone and it fractured our family. Perry and I began having our troubles too. He started traveling with work, lecturing all over the country and was away from home more than he was there. I was having an extremely difficult time dealing with the situation. It affected every part of our lives and there was no getting away from it. Perry tried to deal with it by not being there. As tough as that was, I understood it. I had seen it many times before dealing with patients going through similar situations.

When the boys were both in their teens, they started having frequent and unusual symptoms. These symptoms were different from what we had been dealing with all along. They were having devastating effects on the boys, and the doctors could not make sense of the new problems we were facing. For Reid it was becoming apparent that his "healthier" days were over, and as difficult as it was to face, I was starting to see that things were not going to work out well for him. Eventually Reid was put in the hospital in Boston where his teams of doctors were. I was running back and forth between the kids at home and Reid in Boston. When it became obvious that Reid was dying, I stayed in Boston to be with him. I remember sitting by his bedside on a Monday, looking at him and thinking to myself that he would not be alive by Friday. Sure enough, he died on Friday. After Reid died, I knew I had to drive home and tell the other kids—it was not something I wanted to do on the telephone. When I got to my town I drove past Rob who was walking along the road with some of his friends. He saw me and I pulled over to talk with him. I asked him where he was going and he said he was going to meet up with some friends. Then he said to me, "Mom, I had a dream that Reid died last night, it was awful," he said. I told him to go enjoy himself; I would see him when he got home. I didn't have the heart to tell him then.

Perry was so angry about Reid's death that he did not want any funeral or service whatsoever. I told him that I did not feel right about that and he agreed that we could plant a tree in the garden and bury Reid's ashes there. We went and bought a blue spruce and Perry and I planted the tree in front of our house while the rest of the kids watched from the window. It was an uneventful end to Reid's life and I never felt right about it.

Losing Reid hit us all hard. Rob, Scott, and Pam had an especially hard time with their little brother dying. They were all very close and too young to have to handle something of that nature. Scott, being the oldest boy, had always been a protective and really kind older brother. When either of the boys were not feeling well Scott would stay at home with them and try to entertain them. Sadly, I think he may have felt guilty for being healthy. Eventually, things became too hard for Scott and he started drinking and getting into trouble. We tried to find the answer to dealing with his pain, but he was at that rebellious age and he withdrew from us in every way. It was hard to know what to do; we were all dealing with our own grief. We tried changing his school to get him away from some of the boys he was getting into trouble with. He just found a new group to get into things with.

I think Rob took Reid's death as a warning sign that he had better hurry up. He seemed to live his life at an accelerated pace after that. It was lucky that he did. Within a year of Reid's decline, things started going the same way for Rob. Of course he knew what was coming but he didn't speak about it. When Rob's health started getting worse I decided against Boston's Children's Hospital. I wanted him closer to home, at the hospital where I worked so I could be near him all the time. I am glad I made that decision. If Perry thought anything different, he never said it. At that point Perry and I had been living apart and somewhere around this time I was served with divorce papers. Things had gone from bad to worse and they were not going to get better.

When Rob passed away, it was surreal. I couldn't believe that I had lost both of them in such a short amount of time. This time I insisted we have a service of some sort. Rob had so many friends, I wanted for them to have a chance to say goodbye. I called the principal at his school and asked if we could arrange for the class to come to the house. I wanted to honor Rob in a way that seemed fitting for him. We had the kids that he played music with come and perform a rock concert and everyone stayed over and slept out in tents on the lawn. Rob had a collection of hats and I made sure each of his friends took one to remember him by. It was a beautiful tribute, and if he were there, I know Rob would have loved it. When it was all over I was faced with a harsh reality. Reid and Rob were both gone. Scott, whose problems now included drugs, had left. Perry and I were divorced and the rest of the kids were either in college or on their own. I went from having a home filled to the rafters, to a house that echoed with emptiness. It was devastating.

Scott's troubles continued to get worse and he wandered from one

state to another living life as an addict. He would call home for money once in a while; other than those desperate phone calls, I wouldn't hear from him. I was heartbroken that Scott ended up this way. During the last call I received from Scott, he told me that he had been selling his blood for drug money. He also told me the blood banks would no longer take his blood because he was sick. Having been told by professionals that worked with drug addiction to deal with Scott by using what they called tough love, I told Scott I couldn't send him any more money. I begged him to come home so we could get him the help that he needed. I never heard from him again. My family and I have searched for Scott for many years. He has never been found. Based on our last conversation, I believe either by way of dirty needles, or at the very least by the emotional toll of our family's experience, Scott too lost his life to AIDS.

getting through difficult days

Seeing how difficult it was for Bobby to relive this part of her life was heartbreaking and there were a number of days when shedding tears was a big part of what we both did. During one of those days I asked Bobby how she was able to get through those years. Bobby's eyes squinted with concentration and the pain on her face helped answer the question. "You get through it one day at a time, but you don't ever get over it," Bobby said. "It's hard to describe," she continued, "but when you lose a child it leaves a huge empty space in you that you can't seem to fill. Even now all these years later, I still find myself looking if I see a group of teens around the age my boys were when they died. I know it's not them but I look anyway. Maybe it's to see if I might catch a glimpse of them in another child, or maybe even though I know in my head that they are gone, my heart never really believes it. All I know is that I can see a child that resembles one of my boys, and still shed tears that are almost thirty years old."

As for getting through those difficult years, Bobby told me the following stories about how her healing process began.

Bobby on healing time ...

After the boys died I had a hard time being home. I went from a house full of family to coming home at night and feeling such emptiness. To escape the sadness and loneliness that waited for me each night, I found myself needing to get away. Almost right away I took a trip to Scotland. It was a trip I wanted to take alone and I traveled all across the country. It took six weeks, each place I went and each sight I saw, I told myself that I was doing it for the boys. I decided if they didn't have the chance to see the world, I would do it for them. When I returned from Scotland, I buried myself in my work. It was good that I had a career that never seemed to have a lag because in part that is what saved me. All of my waking hours were devoted to what I could do to ease other people's suffering, yet I had no idea what to do for my own, so I just kept working and traveling. I know it was an attempt to get away from my own life—if I wasn't home maybe I didn't have to remember what my reality was. Of course, that is not how it works.

Since travel was the only solution I could think of, I kept packing my bags and heading off to new places. One day while I was packing and getting ready to take a cruise to Alaska I turned on the news and saw a story about the children in Ethiopia. These children were sick with diseases that here in the States would be taken care of with ease. They were malnourished and their stomachs were distended. They lived in filth and the look in their eyes reminded me of death. It struck me as tragic and

I couldn't get the images of those children out of my mind. When I got onto the ship for my cruise, there was a huge spread of food, everything you could imagine laid out for the passengers. The contrast of what I had seen on the news and what was in front of me ready for consumption was astounding. While on that trip I had a good amount of time to think; what I thought about the most were the children in Africa. Two things seemed to stand out in my mind; the growing numbers of orphans, and AIDS, the disease that seemed to be making them orphans. There was so much to learn about this new disease. It was a very serious plight that the kids in Africa were facing. Because of that I started giving a lot of thought to what could be done about it. Coming home from Alaska I knew that the next trip that I would take would be to Africa. Not only was it where I thought I might look to work on changing the current circumstance, it was a place I had wanted to go since I was a child. I remember sitting by my father as a young girl, listening to the stories told by the missionaries he cared for that had just returned from Africa. I had such a strong desire to go and see what they described that I can even remember getting jealous if one of my sisters would tell me they had dreamt about Africa. I knew the time had come for that trip and even though my reasons for wanting to go had changed, I was hoping the experience could be beneficial to the children of Africa and to me.

On my first trip to Africa I went to see everything I could—the animals, the landscape, and the magnificence that the continent is known for. Again traveling alone, I booked myself on a safari and fishing trip and had the intention of seeing as much as time would allow. Aside from the beauty that I knew I would see, I also wanted to see what life was like there, where the most help was needed and what actually needed to be done. The stark contrast between the beauty and bleakness in that part of the world can be confusing and difficult to process. I saw some of the most beautiful sunsets I had ever seen and at the same time some of the most widespread devastation I had ever seen. I was able to get a good feel for what the children of Kenya were dealing with on that trip: mostly disease, hunger, and loss. AIDS was the highest cause of death and was more prevalent there than anywhere else in the world. Coming home I started

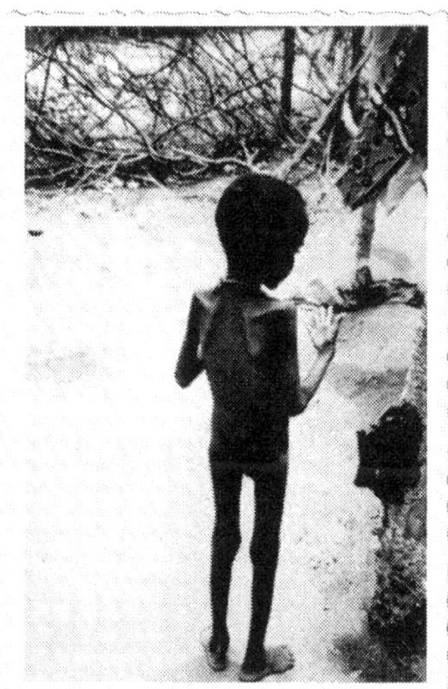

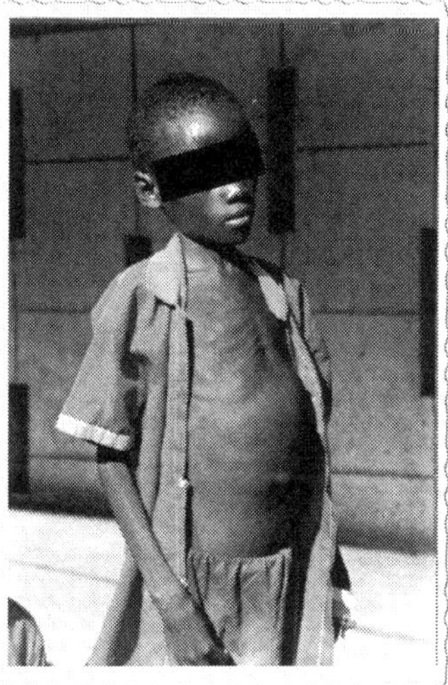

putting my thoughts together on what those children needed. I didn't yet have a plan for how I could help them but I did have the desire and that was a good beginning.

After returning from that first trip, my thoughts were constantly with those children. I didn't really know what to do or how to go about getting help to them, but I knew I needed to try. The thought came to me that I should contact the United Nations and try to get an appointment with the U.N. Ambassador to Kenya. It was easier than I imagined. After calling and explaining my desire to help the people of Kenya, I was given an appointment. On the morning of my appointment I left my house and was about to get into my car when I remembered a photograph I had taken of Rusinga Island in the Lake Victoria region of Kenya. I went back into the house and brought it with me.

Walking into the office of the Ambassador was a bit intimidating. He was a man of about 350 pounds and was about six feet three. That is almost a foot taller than I am and 225 pounds heavier. Sitting across from him I had the feeling that he wondered why I was taking up his time. I went straight into telling him of my visit to the area, what I had seen and what I thought needed to be done. I pulled out the photograph I had taken with me and showed him the area I was interested in focusing on. The photo showed a number of houses in the foreground and Lake Victoria behind the homes. He looked at the picture and a smile spread across his face. Pointing to the only house in the photograph that had a tiled roof he said, "Do you see this house here? That is my mother's house." He picked up his phone, dialed his wife and said, "Prepare another setting at the table; I am bringing home a new friend for dinner." After spending the evening talking with the Ambassador and his wife about their homeland, I knew I had a lot to learn about the area. The Ambassador told me I should go back to Kenya and meet with a nephew of his; he would arrange to have him take me around and teach me everything I needed to know about Rusinga Island and the surrounding areas.

A few months after meeting with the ambassador I returned to Kenya and met up with Oteab, the nephew he had arranged for me to travel with. Oteab was an ambitious young man who had a pleasant way about him. He took his job as my escort very seriously and had arranged for me to see everything. We met with the director of health and we visited all the clinics and hospitals in Kenya. Oteab was the right person to show me around, he was very bright and knew how to get across to people, which much of the time was with the money that seemed to be continually finding its way out of my pockets. That trip cost me $7,000. If I yawned it may have cost me the gold in my teeth—the people there are eager to survive and will without hesitation ask for what they think you might be able to give them. I came away from that trip knowing a lot about Kenya and even more about how the absence of bare necessities can motivate a person to ask for what they need. I also learned how very deeply their needs there ran. I returned from that trip with a mission: I would start getting a plan together to bring aid to the children of this devastated area.

Bobby on finding good in a difficult situation ...

Having covered considerable ground in Kenya on my trip with Oteab, I had found the area requiring the most help was the southwest portion of Kenya, surrounding Lake Victoria. It was there that AIDS and malaria appeared to be taking the greatest toll. Whenever we would visit any of the villages in that area we would always find children, as well as adults, dying from those two diseases. Dr. Rene Brilliant, an excellent pediatrician from Nyack Hospital, was very interested in helping the orphans. We had gotten to know each other quite well during the years that she had cared for Rob and Reid. We both knew we could rely on each other to get a good plan into action and we decided to team up. Together we pooled our ideas and started breathing life into SHARE.

From research I had done about funds being sent to these countries from other governments, I discovered they were not reaching the southwestern Nyanza province. That was the area where they had the biggest problems with public health. AIDS, and the number of orphans existing in that area were increasing by the thousands. It worried me that the funds that were being given to the government did not appear to be used in the areas they were being designated for. We registered SHARE as an NGO (non-governmental organization) to protect our efforts against that. We committed to going out to Kenya and physically seeing that the funds we were raising got into the right hands. We knew SHARE had to be extremely structured and we slowly got a board together. Once we had more people, the ideas really started coming together.

On one of the early visits to Lake Victoria with Dr. Brilliant, we determined that getting functioning clinics up and running would be our highest priority. The extremely high mortality rate of the children was what seemed to be the biggest problem, although there were so many problems. It was obvious that would not be all of what we would need to address. The clinics were a good place to begin because we could start treating people right away. Getting information on the diseases that were prevalent in the area was also highly important because we needed to see what medicines we were going to need to bring back. Besides AIDS and malaria, there were also high incidences of tuberculosis, and a large variety of parasitic diseases. Wound care was also important since burns and injuries from car accidents left a gross number of people in grave condition or dying from things that would be preventable if they were happening in the United States. It quickly became obvious to us that we would need to staff these clinics, and with a limited number of doctors or medically trained people available in Kenya, and our people unavailable for the full-time staffing that was required, we determined an EMS training program was the answer.

Some years earlier, I had started an EMS training program in Rockland County, New York, so I knew what was involved. For starters, we would need a good group of trained EMS technicians from the program back home to go to Kenya. When I got back to New York I approached some of the best technicians and asked if any of them would be interested in teaching the Kenyans how to deal with trauma. The responses came quickly and with enthusiasm. I am still touched by the people who trusted us so early on and willingly jumped on board with us. Keith Rosario, an EMS technician I had worked with for a number of years volunteered to head up the EMS program and I knew it was in good hands. The next item to take on was medical supplies. We started at the local hospitals, getting medical supplies donated, and getting personnel to help. Then we called all the pharmaceutical and drug companies and asked for the drugs we needed. Another big medical problem we had discovered was prevalent in the Lake Victoria region was Burkett's Lymphoma. It is a cancer of the face, neck, and jaw that causes horrific disfigurement; and the number of children that had this cancer was mind-boggling. Aside from getting the drug Cytoxin, which would cure this cancer if treated early enough, we needed to find out what it was that was bringing the incidence of this cancer to such high numbers; next on our plate, a research lab.

At home we had started going around to schools, showing slides of what we were seeing and dealing with in Africa. Some of the images were hard for the kids to look at, especially the images of the children whose faces were nearly eaten away by Burkett's Lymphoma. The images of babies with distended stomachs and small children with barely enough flesh on their bones to keep their skeletons intact were graphic, but we were desperate for help. The children here that saw those images were a great help in raising money for SHARE. Also, from the school talks, we would always get kids that wanted to volunteer their time to help the kids in Africa. A wonderful thing started happening. We (SHARE) were getting a following, and from that came more ideas of how we could raise funds to help our cause. One of our most profitable fundraisers turned into an annual event. We held a Halloween Scare Fair and my home was the setting for the event for seventeen straight years. Since I live in a stone house, it lent itself perfectly to the appearance of a haunted castle. The event became so well known and the turnout so large, that people were coming from other towns and surrounding counties. As news of this event spread we needed to get the local police to direct traffic and keep the flow of things running smoothly, but the event was well-planned and fabulously executed because of the involvement and dedication of our area high school kids.

The Scare Fair became an event not to miss. It served two purposes. The main was to raise money for the AIDS orphans and the health issues in the lake area: but it was a twofold purpose in that it required the participation of a wide variety of people from churches, schools, and clubs of all sorts. Most importantly, it got our children involved in a humanitarian effort that was so sorely needed. It really was a community effort in that it involved radio stations, newspaper, local businesses, and big corporations—all sought after by people in the community, young and old alike. We ran around getting donations from anyone we could think of. There was a lot of begging going on.

CBS somehow heard about the Scare Fair and Dan Rather approached us. A crew came to the fair and became intrigued by the driving force behind it all—SHARE. The next thing I knew, the producer was at my house interviewing me. We talked about my boys and how they had been my motivation to help other children with the disease. They asked if they could send a film crew out to Kenya with us. Luck was certainly on our side. You couldn't ask for better attention than that. So a crew came with us on our next trip and followed us around, recording everything we were doing. We had just given a fair amount of money to Double Joy orphanage and they had used it to build more dormitories for their constantly increasing number of orphans. They had named the buildings after my three boys. I was deeply moved and broke down at the sight of their names hand-written on the front door of each building. It was at that moment that I realized that my boys' lives were making an impact on the lives of other children. It became very clear to me that even though their time was short, and they did not get to experience life to its fullest potential, they had still made a difference.

Even with all the help and press that SHARE was getting, we still needed so much more. The needs were huge in Kenya and we were barely making a dent. I decided I should join a local rotary group and Lion's International. I figured that if there were 1.4 million members in Rotary and 1.2 million members of Lion's, that made 2.6 million people that would have the opportunity to learn about SHARE. That could generate some much-needed noise about the problem of AIDS and the work that we were doing. It was endless, the selling of our cause, and the searching for funds. A lot of people that we approached would say things like, "What about the poor in this country?" All I could tell them was where my drive

SCOTT

to help was coming from. I told them the facts, that there were so many children that were being orphaned because of AIDS and that I was seeing small children barely old enough to be of school age caring for younger siblings. There was nothing for us to do but keep pushing for help and telling as many as we could about the children in Kenya.

My hunch was right about joining rotary. After speaking endlessly about the orphans at one rotary club after the next, a rotary secretary made a call to Lion's International and suggested they should look into the work that SHARE was doing. After hospital rounds one day, I returned to my office to start seeing patients. Madeline, my office manager, told me there was something I would want to see right away on my desk. Curious, I went into my office and found a letter from Lion's International. The letter stated that I had won the Lion's International Award for my work with the children of Africa. With the letter was a check. I was thrilled. SHARE's account had been dwindling, no matter how much fundraising we were doing. This was a much-needed boost. I ran and told Madeline, "I can't believe it; we just were given $20,000 from Lion's International." I hadn't been this uplifted about our efforts for quite some time. Madeline suggested I go back into my office and take a second look at the check. She said, "I think you got some of your zeros mixed up, doctor." With that I could feel some of the excitement drain out of me, I went back into my office expecting to reread the amount on the check at $2,000. Instead what I saw was a check for $200,000. We finally had a real windfall and we could start putting that money to immediate use.

In the southernmost area of Kenya, there was a small town called Sindo. It was a place of abject poverty. Sindo had a hospital that was barely functioning. If given the attention and repair it needed, it could be monumental in helping the people that were suffering in the surrounding areas. However, the current condition of the eight-bed hospital was so poor that it could not meet the needs that were constantly on the increase due to AIDS and malaria. Dr. Misori, the minister of health in Kenya, brought us out to see the hospital. It had such large holes in the roof that when it would rain it would leave large puddles of water everywhere. Although there was a medical officer and several nurses that tried to keep the hospital running, lack of running water and proper lighting made

surgical procedures impossible. The deficiency of supplies and equipment were an obvious problem, but we felt at least it was something to work with and the money we had received from Lion's International could be put to great use if spent there.

We set our goal to get the hospital running and functioning at its highest capability and as quickly as possible. There was a broken down antiquated water pump that was already on site. If repaired we knew it could be used to bring much needed water into the facility from the lake which was only several hundred yards away. Dr. Misori, determined to get the job done, gathered a large group of men and set them about building a pump house. The project was quickly organized and pipes were laid from the lake to the pump house. Then more pipes were run into the hospital buildings. The men also built a kitchen to replace the small closet sized room that had housed a few charcoal pits and served as a primitive kitchen. Also, with the money from Lion's, the roofs of the buildings were replaced and a new operating theater was planned and built with the best operating lights available. Several large generators were purchased and supplies that were donated from the hospitals and drug companies back home were being delivered daily. Everything was painted and large windows were installed to improve the lighting conditions. The transformation was remarkable and word about the hospital was spreading to other villages. An addition to the new facility was an eye clinic, which was extremely important to the community because of the high number of people who suffered from serious eye conditions, including blindness.

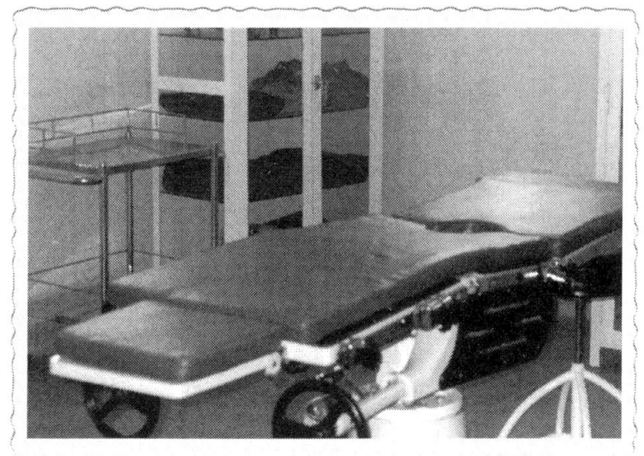

The eye conditions were attributed to untreated infections and to the harsh sun reflecting off of the lake. To commemorate the reopening of the refurbished hospital, the medical personnel and the entire community planned a Harambee—a large celebration in which everyone in the community was expected to contribute by bringing food and donating money. The opening celebration would also include free clinics for all that attended. Dr. Misore invited all the proper guests from the ministry of health and messengers were sent out to the various villages and islands to announce the opening ceremonies and advertise the eye clinic.

When the opening day arrived, boats began to come ashore from the islands. Young school children were sent from various villages in pristine uniforms to sing opening songs and hymns. The ministry of health sent the director of medical services for Kenya, Dr. Richard Muga. Both he and Dr. Misori gave opening addresses and thanked us for our generosity. Over one thousand people arrived for the opening services and for the opportunity to be seen at the clinics. After the opening ceremonies there was a banquet with large platters of fish stews and chicken dishes to feed the attendees. Musicians played while the attendees of the celebration danced, expressing happiness for what this hospital meant for them. The celebration continued for days, as did the lines for the various clinics.

Several of the top eye surgeons from Nairobi and Kissumo were brought in and performed procedures that the people from the islands and small villages had never seen done before. An eighty-six-year-old great-grandfather was the first of the eye patients. He had lost his vision

decades before and had never seen his own grandchildren's faces. The surgeons put in synthetic implants to replace his damaged corneas and his eyes were to remain bandaged for the next 24 hours. When it was time for his bandages to come off, a large crowd had gathered and his wife stood before him with his great grandchildren. The crowd collectively held their breath as the bandages came off and his wife, who was partially blind herself, led his grandchildren up to him. When his eyes opened and he saw his family standing there, tears streamed down his cheeks and the crowd let out a load celebratory roar. It was such an emotional moment for all who were there. The clinics continued on for the next several days until everyone who came, was seen by the medical staff. The hospital had been so desperately needed and it was so well received and appreciated by the people. They were so grateful and happy that even though it was the loss of my own boys that brought me to this far away place I couldn't help but feel joy. Seeing the good we were doing was the start of the healing process for me.

Because of the transformation of the hospital and the success of the opening, we were followed by reporters and the story made the newspapers in Nairobi and Kisumu. We had been in Kenya for a long time because of the amount of work that had to be done to make the hospital opening a success. I was physically exhausted from the work, but the emotional exhaustion may have been even greater. Seeing what we had accomplished was overwhelming at times. After the work was completed, the volunteers from the United States slowly returned home. I went alone to Nairobi to spend a few days finalizing some details with the Ministry of Health. One afternoon, a few days before I was to leave for home, I was resting in my hotel room and a knock came at my door. The man on the other side of the door told me that a call had come in for me from Kenya's President Moi. I was informed that a summons had arrived at the desk for me and that President Moi requested my attendance at the State House. The message said I would be picked up shortly. In a matter of minutes a Mercedes arrived; I was escorted by two huge men in business suits and shoulder holsters to the State House. I couldn't figure out why Moi would want to see me, but it was obvious it wasn't a request that I could refuse.

When I arrived I was taken into a living room and was told to sit and wait. A few minutes later I was moved through three more living rooms. Eventually, I was left in a fourth living room with a tray of tea. Elegant china and silver were next to the tea. Being alone in the room I waited for someone to come in and pour the tea for me—or at least offer it to me. That did not happen. For about thirty minutes I just sat and waited for the next person to come in and move me along. Just outside this room was a long hallway that ended in front of an elaborately decorated pair of gold doors. Once again, someone appeared and I was moved yet again left to sit and wait in the hallway on the outside of the ornate doors. Another twenty minutes passed before a secretary came into the room. He signaled and I followed him to the end of the hall where the doors opened and President Moi was on the other side waiting to greet me. Everything in the room was lavish. The furniture was all gold gilt with red velvet. I went in and waited for him to speak. He motioned for me to sit and then he sat in a chair opposite me. We had an inane conversation for a few minutes and then out of nowhere he said, "I would like to ask you for 1.5 million dollars." With that, a side door opened and a short elegantly suited man with glittering black eyes came into the room and was introduced as Mr. Nicholas Biowatt. He was obviously a chief aid of Moi's and was very somber looking. They spoke of needing the money for some sort of Conservation Park. I was thinking to myself how odd that they were concerned with the conservation of land while there were so many of their people dying.

At this point I was quite uncomfortable and wishing I was on a plane headed home. After some very small talk about what I was doing for the orphans, Moi bluntly came out and asked me again for the 1.5 million dollars; his request was immediately followed by Biowatt asking for an additional one million for some other need. It took the wind out of me. They just assumed that I had money because my photo had been in the paper holding a two hundred thousand dollar check for the hospital in Sindo. I knew I couldn't show any surprise or shock. I had to think quickly. The only thing running around my head at that moment was, What the hell did I get myself into? The second thought I had almost made me laugh out loud. I had all of about $600 in my savings account if I was lucky. I pulled a note pad out of my purse and wrote down the figures on paper with their names next to it. Then I proceeded to tell them that things were sort of scrambled at home financially, but that I *would get to straightening them out as soon as I got home, which as far as I was concerned, was already a day too late. With visions of myself running through four living rooms, and rushing past holster-wearing men, I told them it would probably take me a while to get those kinds of funds together. They asked me for my address in the States; I gave them a fake one. Before I was allowed to go they took me to the garden to have my picture taken with them. I thought that no one at home would believe me when I told them about my little visit with the president, so I figured it would be a good idea to have proof. As soon as our photo session was over I got out of there as fast as I could. After that encounter I wanted so badly to be home that I spent the next two days while I waited for my flight home lying so low that I could have slid under a doormat.*

Returning home was always strange. It would take a while before I would readjust to the differences between our cultures. It was always good to get home but as time would pass my thoughts would always return to what needed to be done in Kenya. With my new friends there keeping me abreast of what those needs were, SHARE kept moving forward. Constantly learning, we would adjust our role based on the needs that were presented. It came to our attention that the numbers of orphans in the area around the lake were increasing daily. It was obvious that our next effort needed to be focused on an orphan sponsorship program.

SHARE's main office was located in Mbita and was situated in Father Tealon's Catholic mission. Father Tealon was a Dutch Catholic priest who had spent his entire adult life in Kenya in the Nyanza province. Within minutes of our first meeting I knew Father Tealon and I would become friends. He had a large family of orphans and administered to a large area of the lakeshore where he had built several churches over the years. He was a true Renaissance man in that he was both architect and builder of his churches, knew a great deal about animal husbandry, was an expert on tree farming and had an incredible truck farming set up which was cared for by the teenaged orphans from his community. He was also a seaman and a sailor. He had a sixty-five foot boat that had been given to him, and he used it to travel to different parts of the lake. Acting as ferry captain, he would pick up people along the way that wished to go from one village to another. The main route was from Mbita to Kisumo and to some of the towns along the northern border of the lake. Father Tealon was a man I felt fortunate to have met and he became a mentor to me. I knew a man who had eleven AIDS orphans living in his home, traveled around the lake preaching at the various boarding schools, spent time visiting sick parishioners, was always available for the christening of babies, and solicited funds from a church flock that was living in poverty, was a man I could learn from. Even though his parishioners were in need themselves, they would always give what they could. Father Tealon was a huge help in getting our orphan sponsorship program operational. I saw through his mission what the orphans needs were and how best to address them. I took what I learned from him back to New York and got to work.

With the need for funds being great, and the obvious realization that it would not be coming from Kenya, we decided the time had come to do some serious fundraising. I had learned something about fundraising from President Moi and his sidekick. Just flat out ask for it. Back in New York I started calling on some of my well-known patients that lived in the small theatrical community along the Hudson River. The first one to respond was Mikhail Baryshnikov. I had met Misha, as he prefers to be called, after he came by my home one Sunday morning with an artist friend of mine. He had his dog Tim with him and I ended up diagnosing a skin condition that the dog had been suffering with. Not long after I advised him on how to deal with Tim's dermatitis, Misha called again. This time it was his personal assistant that was in need of my services. She had opened an Easter gift basket that was sent to Misha at his home and there was an explosive device in the package. It blew up in her face. I spent several hours removing charred bits of paper from her face, neck, and hands. Remembering what I had done for him, Misha was more than willing to help when I called him for assistance.

Baryshnikov and another dance partner held a benefit fundraiser for SHARE in Palm Beach, Florida; the dancers drew a huge crowed and brought in a very successful program. It was our most successful fundraiser and I could never thank him enough for helping us the way he did. After seeing how much someone from the entertainment world could do for SHARE I started reaching out to some of the other actors and theatre people that lived nearby. Ellen Burstyn, although known for her acting, is also a fabulous photographer. She donated a great number of her photographs and we had a gallery showing of her work. The money *we brought in from selling her images was enough to buy a $12,000 solar oven, which we purchased and donated to the village of Mbita. It is still in use and makes enough bread to feed hundreds of people each day.*

Another patient of mine who contributed a great deal to SHARE was Bill Murray, who gave us a generous donation that we were able to use towards building dispensaries on the lakeshore that we found were necessary to keep our mobile clinics running smoothly. Helen Hayes was always a wonderful supporter of SHARE and helped considerably in making it a successful venture. It is nice being able to look back and revisit the generosity of all of those people and I hope they realized how much their efforts were appreciated by the AIDS orphans in Kenya and me. When you make a difference in a child's life, especially one that means the difference between life and death, it is something that lasts their entire lifetime. I always like to think about what those children have done with the gifts they were given.

One of the things that brought me great pleasure through the years is the generosity and hard work of our children here at home. It is because of them and their efforts that the sponsorship program became a success. Going around to schools when I was not in the operating room or seeing patients was the best way to get a surge of funds. After seeing the images of the orphan children our kids would be deeply moved by the contrast they saw between their own lives and the lives that the orphans were living. It was so easy for them to feel the urgency to help after seeing children suffering. As SHARE grew, and all the new programs seemed to fall into place, I have always felt fortunate and grateful for the support we received from the wonderful and generous people who have worked with us. As new needs arose, we were always able to meet the challenges and I know it would not be so if it were not for the people who joined with us. Whether it was members of SHARE's board or members of the community, like the high school students, their teachers, the local medical community, big corporations, EMS technicians, members of the local police, or fire departments, people were always willing to help. I truly believe that when you are asking for something from your heart, something that is selfless and will benefit those in need, you will get the positive response that is needed. It is human nature to care for each other.

CHILDREN'S
HOSPITAL
EDUCATI
NYACK HOSPITAL

doing good and getting better

By reaching out and helping others, Bobby was able to extract something good from the most difficult situation imaginable. First in the "quality of life" changes that she brought to the children of Kenya, and then in her own healing process that came as a direct result of the good she was doing. I am convinced that Bobby was only able to survive the loss of her boys because of what she was doing for other people's children. After hearing Bobby speak of those difficult days with her boys and after seeing the pain she still felt when she relived those days, I can't comprehend how she managed to do what she did in Kenya, but I do know that it is what keeps her going. It is why at eighty-five years old, she still needs to do it. I don't know anyone that has suffered on the level that Bobby has. I suppose that makes her an authority on the subject of recovery. Using her grief as a vehicle to help others, Bobby was able to reclaim her life. In a sense, she became her own healer and that suggests to me that although she may have not have found a cure for grief ... she certainly found an effective treatment for the unfairness of tragedy.

I learned a great deal from Bobby on the matter of healing. After my accident I found the thing that was most painful for me were the regrets I was carrying around. With my voice temporarily silenced by my broken jaw, my mind seemed to want to speak up. The thing it was saying most often was that I had been foolish in the passive approach I had taken to my own life. What bothered me the most about that—was it was not something I could change; the years had passed and I had let them. I was pretty annoyed with myself about that. Of course, talking to Bobby about her life always led to reflection on my own. One day Bobby and I were discussing how she had been able to continue helping others after going through what she had with her boys. I wanted to know how she was not bitter, how she was not living in a state of anger for what happened in her life. Bobby said, "There really is no point in being angry or regretful about something that you cannot change. It doesn't help the situation. The only thing you have control over when you are faced with something unpleasant is how you react to it. I felt it would be more useful to see what I could do so that others did not have to experience what my boys and my family went through." Another lesson learned! I decided right then to put my regrets where they belonged—in the past. I also began to realize that it was those very regrets that put me where I was now. Suddenly it was easy to change how I reacted to them!

In recent years Lyme disease has forced Bobby into retirement and a disabled hip has kept her from going back to Africa on SHARE's most recent missions. Seeing how easily pain can creep back into her heart when she has too much downtime has made it clear to me how important it is for Bobby to keep doing what she enjoys most: making a difference in the lives of others. I feel extremely fortunate to be spending this time working with Bobby and delivering the valuable lessons her life story offers. I am grateful for the trust that she put in me to make sure that this book would not just be a summary of events that took place in her life, but more a useful road map to stay with the reader until the time might come when they find one of her stories useful for their own journey.

The work that Bobby is doing now may be different than the hands on work she is used to doing, but it is just as valuable. By sharing her story, by speaking and by writing this book, Bobby is still helping others. Based on the reactions and standing ovations she gets when we finish a school program, I would say the messages that Bobby delivers are being well received. Bobby's story offers priceless lessons to carry forward in life. Hearing what she has been able to accomplish in her lifetime despite so much adversity makes you want to figure out your own way to make a difference. I know it has for me. Which leads us to the next part of this journey.

Anne Nielsen

Symptom:

I have had some very difficult situations in my life.
I don't know if I will ever get over
what I have had to deal with.
How do you move on from that?

Name——————————— Date————

Address ———————————————

Rx

You have two choices when you have experienced something dfficult. You can give in to it and let it destroy you- or you can find a way to turn it around to help others who may be worse off than you are. I can assure you that by choosing option two you will end up in a better place.

Signature *Martha M. MacGuffie, MD*

Symptom:

I want to help others who have gone through similar challenges as mine but I don't know where to find them or what I can do for them.

Name Date

Address

Rx

You can find people with needs everywhere. Find a way to use what you are good at as a starting point for how you can help them.

Signature *Martha M. MacGuffie, MD*

Symptom:

I can't get past the anger and resentment that I have over the difficult situation I have had to face.

Name ________________ *Date* ______

Address ________________

Rx

There is no point in being angry or bitter about something that you can not change. The only thing that you can do is change how you react to it. Your choice will determine whether you regain control of the direction you want your life to go.

Signature Martha M. MacGuffie, MD

lesson three

Lynn Cluess Manzione

one person

Bobby's father always told her that one person can make a difference. It's fairly obvious that for Bobby, her father's words became the seeds to grow on. When I think about this statement I can't help but wonder if her father had any idea of how many different ways his daughter would prove those words to be true. After seeing what Bobby had accomplished in some of the most difficult situations, I had to ask her if she ever felt overwhelmed by the enormity of a situation she was about to delve into. I wanted to know if there was ever anything that had scared her off; if there was ever anything this woman found was too large to take on. As I asked, of course I had my reasons for wanting to know her answer. You see, spending time around Bobby does not allow a person to remain idle. You can't take in the enormity of what she has accomplished and expect that your life will continue on as it was before you met her. You have to figure out what it is that you can do. You just must, and you want to. Bobby is like lighter fluid; she can ignite a flame in anyone. Ideas were coming to me all the time but, of course, I had my usual doubts to overcome first. Fortunately, I also had Bobby to bounce my crazy thoughts off of. Funny thing, Bobby never seemed to see them as crazy. While I prefaced each potential scheme with "I know this sounds crazy," and "I don't know if this is possible but ..."

Bobby replied to each one with, "Why not," or "You can do anything you set your mind to." This was going to take a radical change in thinking for me but I slowly started to see what Bobby knew. If you wanted to make something happen, you have to be willing to jump in without knowing the outcome. Bobby's answer to my question of whether there was ever anything she felt too big to take on spoke on the subject of boldness ...

Bobby on the importance of boldness ...

One day a page in the hospital came for me just as I stepped out of the operating room. Helen Hayes was on the phone and she wanted to know if I was free to come over for a cup of tea and to meet a gentleman that was sitting in the living room of her Nyack home. He was there asking her for a donation and wanted to know if she would be a spokeswoman for an organization he had founded called AmeriCares. At the time I was at the very beginning stages of getting SHARE started. Knowing that I had traveled to Africa and was in the process of working with the hospital to bring much needed medical aid to Lake Victoria, Helen figured I would be a good judge of this man's character.

When I walked into her living room and saw him sitting there in that blue sweater, his big frame looking so out of place on her delicate sofa, I couldn't help but smile. I had already told myself I would meet this man. Only about a month earlier I had read an article about him. In the photo that accompanied the article he wore that same blue sweater. Standing up, he introduced himself to me. "Hello, I'm Bob Macauley," he said.

I answered him with, "I know who you are, and just so you know, we were supposed to meet." The confused expression on his face matched the one on Helen's face.

"What do you mean we were supposed to meet?" he asked. "Did we have an appointment that I failed to make?" was his next question.

I explained that I had read the recent magazine article about him and just after putting it down, I said aloud to myself, "I am going to meet that man." I couldn't explain it; it was something I felt in my bones. I knew that a man that had done what Bob Macauley had done was someone I wanted to know.

In 1975 Bob was deeply affected when he heard about 243 Vietnamese orphans that had been gathered by American aid workers and loaded onto a United States Air Force C-5A. It was an effort to get the children out of the dangerous war-ridden area of Vietnam and to the safety of the United States, but, twenty minutes after taking off, the plane crashed and over one hundred of the children were killed. If that wasn't bad enough, the other devastating news was that getting another Air Force plane to the survivors would take at least ten days. Knowing that by then it would be too late to help those children, some of whom were suffering from serious burns and injuries, Macauley, a paper manufacturer, wrote a personal check and put his home up as collateral. He then chartered two Pan Am 747s to get the kids and bring them back to the United States where they could be adopted and begin a new life. The end result was … the planes got there and brought the children back to the United States … his check bounced and he lost his house. Bob felt that was a fair price to pay knowing that he had saved the lives of all those children. After the article was published he started receiving donations from all sorts of places and fortunately was able to recover his home. The feeling it had left him with motivated him to continue helping those in need. That is how AmeriCares began. In the twenty- some-years since that time, Bob and his organization have been able to raise and donate over 8 billion dollars in aid and have helped people in need all over the world.

After the first meeting in Helen's living room, Bob and I became fast friends. One of the first things he did for me was to take me to see his good friend Bill Simon. Bill had been treasurer under President George Bush, senior. Bob told Bill of what I had been trying to get done in Kenya and asked if he thought he could help finance some of what I was trying to get accomplished. Then Bob told his friend about my premonition. He told him he believed our chance meeting was actually destiny. Bill Simon must have gotten some good vibes from me because he turned around and wrote Bob a personal check for $150,000 to be used towards SHARE. With that kind of money I knew we could get a lot done in the Lake Victoria area. I also knew that when someone goes out of their way to do something for you on that level you tend to feel indebted. Not that Bob himself made me feel that way, it was just the act of trust and generosity that had come from him that made me want to do whatever I could to repay him. The opportunity would come up more than once. Over the years Bob's organization AmeriCares had grown considerably and they were doing work all over the world. If there was a need somewhere for humanitarian effort, Bob and AmeriCares were involved. It wasn't long after I first met him that the opportunity to repay his favor would arise. Whenever those opportunities presented themselves I would always do what I could for Bob and his causes. Some of the efforts he was involved in seemed hopeless, but as I learned from Bob Macauley, when one person *joins with another in an effort to better a situation the solution will come. Eventually the number of people willing to be a part of the solution will grow large enough to have an impact.*

Bob Macauley Founder of AmeriCares

During the genocide in Rwanda in 1994, AmeriCares was sending medical personnel to join the relief effort under the United Nations High Commission for Refugees (UNHCR). Bob called and asked if I would lend my skills as a surgeon. In less than two days I had my staff rearrange all of my scheduled surgeries and office visits. I packed a minimal amount of clothing, lots of peanut butter and jelly, and boarded a plane that took off from JFK Airport in New York and headed to Amsterdam. Also on that trip were Dr. Rene Brilliant and EMS technician Keith Rosario. From sources I don't recall, we were given a bicycle with a pull cart attached to be used for local transportation when we arrived at our destination. After arriving in Amsterdam we immediately began the task of gathering whatever supplies we were going to need. The bike's pull cart came in handy because by day's end we had filled it to capacity with items we had collected from various sources. The next leg of the trip would take us from Amsterdam to Goma, Zaire. There was an American camp there and that was where we would be working. Before being delivered to the camp clinics, we stayed a few days in a non-functioning town that was flooded with French soldiers. Our purpose for being there was a sort of orientation with UNHCR. Our housing for that time was a deserted barroom with mattresses spread from wall to wall.

While we were there, a group of civilians that had been caught in a bloody battle had found their way to our doorstep. A number of them were in desperate need of surgery and there was no place but the barroom to perform those surgeries. The conditions were obviously less than ideal. With no electricity we knew we would need to get set up close to the windows. The floor was not an ideal set up for performing surgeries so I told the man who seemed to have charge over the bar that we would need to find tables and have them brought over to the windows. The man looked me in the eye and said, "I really like you boots, doctor." I couldn't understand why he was talking about my boots when there were people that were in obvious pain, with injuries that required immediate attention. Annoyed and frustrated, I explained again what I needed to be done with the tables. This time he stood silently with a smile on his face. His eyes went from mine to my boots and back to my eyes again. His words were not needed; I finally got what he was saying to me. I took off my boots and slid them towards him. In a matter of seconds they were on his feet. Without delay he began rushing around and calling out to other men to bring me the tables I had requested. I learned quickly how things got done in this place. Barefoot, I stood next to a table placed closely to a window and set about my work.

When we were finally brought into the refugee camp I was completely overwhelmed by the number of displaced children there were. I remember stepping out of the car and looking out at an endless sea of people. It is estimated that there were over 750,000 refugees in that camp. The numbers grew daily with the influx of refugees that came over the border into Kenya and formed one of the largest camps in sub-Saharan Africa. Living in the camp for the six weeks that followed, I got a genuine feel for their existence.

Days at the refugee camp were long. I would wake up at 6 a.m. and go to the medical tents to begin my day. The hospital tents were filled with people with serious needs. They would come one after the next and there would be no stop to seeing patients except for a short afternoon break. After that we would work on until after dark. We (the American camp) had a large clinic that had a continuous line of refugees needing treatment for malaria, malnutrition, respiratory diseases, tuberculosis, AIDS, cholera, and wound care. The medical tents were set up by country. The American clinic was between the French and the Israeli clinics and the relations between them were very good. We would exchange supplies and goods when either group had a particular excess of something. Each compound or tent was set up to handle a particular type of need. We had a preponderance of surgeons and orthopedic specialists. The Israelis had a large rehabilitation set up for post trauma. The French were set up to treat infectious diseases. We would exchange patients and specialists according to need and we all worked very well together. We would also exchange supplies, swapping body casts for sterile sponges or IV drugs for surgical supplies.

At the center of this huge compound was a large one-story brick building that had at one time been a children's school. That building served as our headquarters. It had a high wall around it that provided some safety. We also received protection from local police and soldiers, but in general we were not seeing the fighting, just the result of it. The children who were injured or sick were kept in the brick building on blankets, which were spread over the hard concrete floor. There was no electricity; so again, we set up for surgery right next to a large window, which had abundant light for illumination. When the afternoon rains would fall it became very difficult to see and in the night we would not attempt to do any procedures at all except for extreme emergencies. In those instances we had some battery-powered lighting that we would work with. It was a difficult situation, and for doctors that had come from facilities where working conditions were ideal, it opened our eyes to how fortunate not only we were, but also how fortunate our patients at home were. After the children were well enough to be moved, we would transfer them to the white tents supplied by the UN, which were set up just outside of the building within the compounds protective walls.

At the height of the refugee crisis, there were so many coming into the clinics and the things that were claiming most lives were cholera and battle wounds. Given the vast number of people we were treating, we of course had a large number that did not survive. In those instances we were faced with the issue of disposing of bodies. Bodies were not allowed to be burned, and most of the loose dirt and softer soil had blown away so burying them was impossible. The earth that was left behind was hard baked clay that had been cleared of all brush and foliage to be used as fuel. Bodies of some of the small children were put in rows in shallow graves and then covered with stones. I remember being told as a child that storks brought babies to waiting mothers and fathers. We all have that picture in our minds when we think of the stork. A smiling diapered baby swinging from the sling carried in the stork's beak. In that picture the stork gently releases the child down the chimney of a happily awaiting family. In the shallow graves at camp Magungu in Zaire, the storks were better known for scavenging the flesh off the bones of the dead children that were placed in those shallow graves. Horrific sights were everywhere and for the most part needed to be ignored when it was clear that there was nothing that could be done about them. If you didn't ignore them and keep moving, you would never accomplish anything.

There was an extinct volcano right near our camp. Military groups were left with the unpleasant task of disposing of the large numbers of dead. The decision was made that the bodies would be plowed into the crater of the extinct volcano. It was a horrible sight to see, but there were no other feasible options. One day, while we were on our rounds, the soldiers were in the process of disposing of the bodies; most of whom had been killed by either cholera or machine gun fire. I can vividly remember one woman lying dead, staring blankly skyward at the edge of the crater. The sight of this particular woman stood out because she had her arms wrapped around a small child that was lying across her chest. The plow was heading toward her body and she was about to be pushed over the edge into the pile of corpses. Keith, our paramedic from New York, noticed the child move and ran out in front of the plow waving his arms frantically for the driver to stop. Rushing to the child, he grabbed her out of harm's way. He rushed the baby girl into the hospital clinic and we examined her for injuries.

The child appeared to be about 18 months old. When we examined her, we found that she could not stand. Further investigating led us to a wound in her left hip. The only anesthesia available was local anesthesia, which we injected into the area after it was cleaned. Keith had noted charring around the margins of the wound, which we then explored. I extracted a fifty-caliber machine gun bullet from the wound, which we later found out was the same bullet that had passed through her mother's chest, killing the mother and wounding the baby she courageously tried to protect. The little girl was brought to the main building after the surgery to recuperate, and in a matter of days she was up and running around the clinic. We named her Boom-Boom, and she became a ray of sunshine in a place that was filled with darkness. We all fell in love with Boom-Boom and one of the nurses from Zaire adopted her. Thankfully, there were occasionally stories with happy endings and we clung to those. As a reminder of the child and the difficult days in Zaire, I kept the bullet we extracted from her hip and had it bronzed. I wear it to this day on a chain around my neck. Some things just shouldn't be forgotten. I will never forget those days and I will never forget Keith Rosario in Zaire. It was such a horrible time and his true value as a human being came out to me on that trip.

The missions that I worked with AmeriCares grew to a fair number, and always when the time was done and I prepared to return home, I would leave without the satisfaction of knowing that we finished what we came for. Sadly, our leaving was not about completion, it just meant a new crop of doctors were needed, ones that were fresh. I would return home drained with images of the refugees constantly in my mind. With the visual aid of the suffering that I had witnessed while in Rwanda, and the enormity of what was needed in that part of the world, I was even more committed to getting something accomplished with SHARE. I knew that we couldn't help them all but that we could certainly make an impact. In Rwanda I saw that if one person joins with another and then another and so on, a great deal can be done. That is what makes a task that would otherwise seem unattainable somewhat more manageable and a lot less overwhelming. What I also learned from Bob Macauley, was that sometimes, you need to go forward even when you are facing the unknown. Being bold enough to take action is part of what is needed when you are trying to accomplish something large and bring about something better.

what can I do?

As **Bobby was telling me this** story my eyes were locked on her face. Her eyes had drifted off and I could see that she was in that moment, reliving the experience. The look on her face was pained and I felt bad that I brought her back to that time and place. Even though she was sitting safely in the home that she loves, I could see how uncomfortable those memories were making her. I started thinking about the number of other memories that Bobby owned that could bring about that kind of upset. Even though those days were difficult and reflecting on them brought pain, I knew Bobby felt they served a purpose. At this point I also knew her well enough to see how difficult it was for her to have the idle time that her days were now filled with. Wanting to get her mind off of those thoughts, I asked Bobby what else she hoped to do that she had not yet done. Her answer once again showed me the importance of contribution in her life. Bobby thought for a moment and said, "My boys' lives were short. ..." Again, her eyes focused on something beyond what my eyes could see. She spent a moment lost in thought and then continued; "It would be nice to know their memory could live on and that their existence could have an impact on the lives of others." At that moment, my heart, which was already filled with love for Bobby, expanded to make room for more. It took all the strength that I could muster to hold in the tears that had forced their way to the corners of my eyes. With all that Bobby has done for me, and the positive changes in my life because of her, my mind began racing with thoughts about what I could do so that this could happen. I knew creating something that would benefit children would be the most satisfying for Bobby. Bobby once again was on to something. Her boys' memory could live on through the act of helping others. Bobby and I began to talk about the possibilities of starting a foundation. Not a foundation that would offer financial support, but more in line with what Bobby has always believed: offer our young people the tools they need to achieve their goals through educational programs and mentoring; have programs where they can utilize their talents to help others. For Bobby, one of the saddest things about her boys dying at such an early age was that they never had the chance to leave their mark on the world. If the MacGuffie Foundation could help others do this, to Bobby, it would mean her boys' lives had meant something.

For all of this to come to be, I knew it would take tremendous planning and we would need to get funding from somewhere, but if we could make this happen we could continue to promote the principles handed down by Bobby's father. The principles that have not only made Bobby who she is, but, in addition, have so positively affected the people she has touched throughout her lifetime. I had already seen the constructive effect we were having on the kids we were speaking with; I knew this was a worthwhile cause. I also knew it was going to be a huge task to accomplish and one that needed to be done for Bobby, not by Bobby. Even though the ideas for the programs were flowing, I had no idea where to start the process of forming a foundation, raising the kind of money we would need or any and everything else that would come up with taking on a project of this nature and magnitude. I might not have the know-how yet, but I have the desire, and that's a good start. I do know that my time spent with Bobby has left me with the need to find my own way to contribute and I can't think of a better outcome than for it to be a way to foster the importance of living life to its fullest, and, to honor her and her boys as well.

After many hours filled with thoughts of how enormous this task was and how little I knew about getting something like this done, Bobby once again offered the answer—this time without having to say a word. This time through the pages of notes and stories that were already sitting on my computer. Thinking about what Bobby has accomplished, I realized I already had the blueprint for bringing something like this to life within the pages of Bobby's story on the subject of getting SHARE off the ground. All I needed was to make the decision that I would do whatever was necessary to try to make it happen. Making that decision was easy. Bobby has earned a payback and she most certainly deserves it. Of course, I would never have dreamed of taking on a task of this magnitude if it were not for my time spent with Bobby. Bobby has transformed me into a fearless woman who now believes that most anything is possible if you believe enough in it and work hard enough at it. I am looking forward to what will come of that.

The time that I have spent with Bobby has allowed for me to see the amount of love there is for her not only here in our community but across the globe as well. I hope writing this book and sharing what Bobby has done with her time on this planet will generate more of that. When that happens I know we will have what will be needed to make the foundation a success. In the end when we have the reward that only a heartfelt effort could bring, we will have a Harambee and celebrate the foundation coming to be, and in doing that we will celebrate our love for a woman who has on countless occasions shown us hers.

the subject of fate and faith

Of **the many questions** that I have put forth to Bobby, the next one came after much reflection on the set of circumstances that brought me to my current place in life. It came from a curiosity that was persistently bubbling to the surface no matter how many times I pushed it away. It was a question that had to do with fate and wondering if it was something other than my own choice that had placed me in Bobby's life and decided my new course. Call it faith or religion or God or a higher power or the universe or whatever you like. The question was coming up because I wanted to know how or why I had ended up on this journey at this point in my life or in Bobby's for that matter. How did it just so happen that we both should meet at just the right times in our lives? One more time Bobby's response seemed to satisfy my question. "I don't know what it is or what it is not," she said. "I can only say that it seems there is something that is with us that guides us on our journey. Maybe it's angels." Yes, I thought, maybe it is!

a revelation

I **went to a parochial school** for the first five years of my education. During that time in my life I spent a full year in the classroom of an elderly nun that spent more of her time beating us up physically, verbally, and mentally than she did on any curriculum. I did learn a great deal from her, however. The day she berated me in front of my classmates and hurled my black and white composition book at me Frisbee-style for not capitalizing a sentence, I learned that some people that were supposed to be representatives of God could actually seem more like the devil. I learned that again and again as I watched the brutal actions she brought upon child after child that year. I guess you could say she scared the heaven out of me—doing a thorough job of obliterating the need for any religious beliefs in my life. Because of her I never gave much thought to the notion of a higher power being present in my life. In actuality, I would say I had decided to be a non-believer.

Over the years, several things happened in my life that were directly related to that woman and should have been cause for me to re-evaluate those thoughts. First occurred during a writing class I was taking as an adult many years removed from that nun's classroom. We were given an in-class assignment in which we were asked to describe a person from our past walking through the door of our classroom. In a nanosecond, my mind invited Sister Fidelis and my pen never paused. When I finished the assignment and read my memory of my fourth grade teacher to the rest of my class, the woman sitting across from me (who was easily thirty years older than I was) was noticeably uncomfortable. As I described the experiences that my classmates and I had endured in Sister Fidelis' classroom, I couldn't help but notice the woman squirming uneasily in her chair. When I finished sharing my piece, which did not include the name of the nun or the school, the squirming woman turned to me and asked, "By any chance was the name of the nun you just described Sister Fidelis, because you just brought me back to my fifth grade classroom!" Evidently, I was not the only one that carried the experience of that woman with me. That nun had decades to work her wickedness and sadly a large number of innocent children to do a job on.

Flash forward several decades. I walk into my five-year-old son's school on his first day of kindergarten. Standing in the hallway is a teacher that I recognize. She is my art teacher from my days in that same parochial school. She is the one that made attending school bearable in those days. Almost thirty years have passed, but she is still smiling and greeting the young children she will be left charge over with warmth and kindness. I am so pleased to see her that I walk up to her and ask her if she remembers me. Not only does she remember me, she remembers my brother Nicholas; she remembers that my father was a New York City police officer; she remembers my mother. I want to grab her and hug her. I feel great relief knowing that my son will spend time in her presence. Fortunately, Mrs. Giraldi would come to teach both of my sons before her time to retire arrived. When that time did arrive, I asked my old teacher if she would come out of retirement temporarily to work on an art project in my home with my children and me. Thankfully, she agreed, and for several months she would come once a week. One day, she and I got into a conversation about Sister Fidelis. Mrs. Giraldi not only had worked at the school but she had been very active in the parish and volunteered her time in the nun's residence. After telling her about the devastating memories I had of my time in Sister Fidelis's classroom, Mrs. Giraldi told me a story. She said that when a nun would die, their photograph would be placed in a display case in the convent in honor of their memory. With it would be a special item that had belonged to that nun. Next to Sister Fidelis's photograph was a letter of apology, which was found after her death and was written to all of her students for any harm she may have caused them. For me that was useful information to have, and it allowed me to realize that some of the things that you carry around should be let go. Looking back to the days in her classroom I can recall many stories Sister Fidelis shared about her childhood. I can look at those stories now and realize she suffered abuses of her own. We all carry baggage with us. It is best to realize where it comes from and to get a handle on it so it doesn't continue to affect not only our lives, but also the lives of others we may eventually come to influence. I know one thing for sure: teachers offer immense value on many levels, to many lives. Every child is influenced by at least one teacher, be it in the classroom or in life. Those who realize their influence and foster the best in those they guide are our heroes. They do not live behind the glass of a television screen and we should not see them as if they are enshrined in some trophy case set there to be admired. What we should see when we look at a hero is the empty space that is next to them waiting to be filled.

As I look back now at the chain of events that have taken place not only in my time spent with Bobby, but in the way my life has gone in general, I can't help but feel that everything happened in the time and space it was meant to happen in. I am convinced that all of the things that took place in my life, that brought me to where I am right now, were guided by a force much greater than me or my desires. I am happy and comforted to know that this experience has also taught me that there is another presence that will be with me on the rest of my journey. For me, that makes one more thing to be thankful for. Another silver lining.

This book has changed shapes many times since its inception. It has had many starts and stops. In the end, it has allowed for time to pass and for strangers to become good friends and I am so grateful for that. Bobby, your journey has touched, and continues to touch, so many. I need you to know that it hasn't just been the orphans and people of Kenya, or the 50,000 patients that you have treated during your fifty-year career that you have benefited. You have changed who I am and made me into a person who wants to be sure my time here positively touches the lives of others ... because I now understand that is the point of our being here.

So Bobby, where has this journey taken me? What souvenir will I treasure most? Which ones am I eager to re-gift with the purpose of perpetuation? Why was it that this opportunity found me at just the right moment in life? These questions are not really the important ones. It is the question of how far the gifts that you offer can go that is. Through the people you have touched in your lifetime I see them going on forever. Bobby, several times along the way you and I have agreed that we met for a reason. Clearly we were wrong ... we have met for many. Thank you, Bobby, for all you have done ... all you are still doing ... and all you are yet to do!

With friendship, love, and purpose,

Lynn

Symptom:

I want to get involved in a cause
but I don't know where to begin.

Name——— Date———

Address ———

Rx

Begin with your heart. Figure out what you are drawn to and then decide what actions need to take place to start the ball rolling.

Signature *Martha M. MacGuffie, MD*

Symptom:

What can I do to get involved with SHARE or the MacGuffie Foundation?

Name —————— Date ——

Address ——————

Rx

You can find information about
SHARE at
www.shareafrica.org

You can find information about
The MacGuffie Foundation at
www.macguffiefoundation.org

Signature *Martha M. MacGuffie, MD*

Symptom:

I have a cause that I would like
to get off the ground.
How should I go about getting it started?

Name Date

Address

Rx

Clarify what it is you want to accomplish.
Research what is already availble.
Join community organizations and talk to everyone you meet about what it is you want to achieve.

Signature Martha M. MacGuffie, MD

the assignment

what will you do?

"What lies behind us, and what lies before us, are tiny matters compared with what lies within us."

—Ralph Waldo Emerson

So this is where you enter the picture. Why would you choose to just settle in life? Why should you succeed if your efforts are small? Why would you let fear or failure be your reason to quit? Who should believe in you, if you don't believe in yourself? What will you do to live your life to its fullest? How will your journey turn out?

What makes you feel like you are on your life's path? What will you change so that it is the path that you take? How much of an effort are you willing to make? What will you do to live your life to its fullest? How will your journey turn out?

How will you react when you are faced with a challenge? What voice will you listen to when the travel gets rough? How will your reaction bring about something better? What will you do to live your life to its fullest? How will your journey turn out?

How can you see to it that your time here will matter? How will it matter to somebody else? What will you do to see to it that happens? Why should you get, if you are not willing to give?

What will **YOU** do to live **YOUR** life to its fullest? How will **YOUR** journey turn out?

Your life is going to be what you make of it. Along the way you will meet your teachers. Be alert, pay attention and learn from them.

Here are some simple things you can do to get your life headed in the direction that you want to take it. You can do them and start getting to that place or you can close this book and let life take you where it may. If you are ready to start taking it where you want it to go, turn the page and start doing the things you need to do to get you where you want to go.

Figure out what it is that you do want by seeing what you have that you don't want. (Do the left hand column first.)

What I have in my life that I do not want	What I want in my life that I do not have

From the list on the previous page pick the ten most important things that you do want. Then take on one at a time and get to work. (When you complete this list make a new one.)

1.
2.
3.
4.
5.
6.
7.
8.
9.
10.

The Six Things That I Will Accomplish Today

Item 1 ______________________	Item 2 ______________________
Item 3 ______________________	Item 4 ______________________
Item 5 ______________________	Item 6 ______________________

In each box, in order of priority, write what you commit to accomplishing today. Make sure they are things that will move you closer to your goal. Write what you need to do to achieve these items and get to work. Do not start on your next item until you have completed the one before it. Do this every day and you will succeed at what you set out to accomplish.

epilogue

In high school I played basketball. We were a tight-knit bunch back then, the definition of the word team. But as it goes, life took each member of our group in a different direction, and we lost track of each other through the years. Despite present-day cyber-tools such as e-mail and Facebook—time's passage had put us out of contact. One e-mail changed all of that. It came from a teacher that had made the kind of impression on me that teachers are supposed to make. She was the coach of that high school team, who decades ago, moved too many miles away. She was the one who encouraged me to dream big—the one I had ignored. Having summer plans to travel back our way, she wrote and asked if I might be able to gather some of the old team together for a reunion of sorts. One by one, I located members of that group. One by one

I called, left messages and invited them to gather. One by one they said yes. Truthfully, I was really not sure how comfortable that get-together would be. So many years had passed. Were any of us still who we used to be?

My fear of the awkward strain of getting through that night dissolved the instant we all said hello. We were all who we used to be—old friends, with that bond and connection that teammates have. That one night was all it took to rediscover friendships that I had almost forgotten. We vowed to stay connected. We kept our word.

As with so much else that has occurred since my journey with this project began, a question kept coming back to me: Why? Why was it that at this time, while I was searching for the answer of how I could get this foundation to happen for Bobby, these people re-entered my life? I knew the answer to this question. It was because I knew them. It was because I could trust them. It was because I could rely on them. We were a team once before and I felt that we could be a team once again.

A dinner to celebrate the coming of a new year and a new decade was planned. I knew it would be a great time to ask them if they would want to get involved. I was asking for a lot from a group who had little to do with each other for a large number of years. I pitched my idea at dinner and asked them all to think about it and e-mail me after they had time to digest it. Over the next few days, while I waited for their answers, I calculated exactly how many years had passed since we last were a team. The number was thirty-three—the same number that I wore on the basketball court where we first learned how to work together.

One by one their answers came in. "I will be the first to say that I am in on this project." … "Let me be the second to jump in and say yes." … "I am in." … "Yes." … "I too am in." … "Let's get this ball rolling." … "I'm in, think this will be great." … "I am down with this project wherever, whenever and however it evolves." …

So here is where the book ends—and what a wondrous journey it has been!

It is also where a new journey begins. I can't think of a better way to start it than with old friends.

post epilogue

seven years post the original

I am sorry to say that although the original epilogue played out quite well on paper, our good intentions with the MacGuffie Foundation did not.

Although the renewed friendships from the old days thankfully remain, my dream for Bobby's house, nor Bobby herself have survived. Both dream and friend gone. And my favorite dog Pepper too. Gone- but all remembered, cherished, and important parts of my own wondrous journey.

Strange things happen, and sometimes the most well intentioned plans do not work for reasons unclear to us. That is until they become clear. SHARE Africa continues under amazing leadership hand picked by Bobby. Usha Wright, Jerry Warshaw, and the SHARE board have done and continue to do amazing things for the people of Kenya. I was blessed to have the opportunity to join SHARE's board for a time and travel to Kenya where I met many of the people Bobby spent time with. That experience gave me clarity. It's now my mission to keep Bobby's story alive, so she can continue her work. Although my hopes for The MacGuffie Foundation came from my heart, it was not to be. Dare I say EVERYTHING happens for a reason.

Author's Note

The portions of this book written in the voice of Dr. Martha MacGuffie were as recalled and relayed to Lynn Cluess Manzione by Dr. Martha MacGuffie.

The portions of this book written in the voice of Lynn Cluess Manzione are based on her own opinions and interpretations.

Eighty-five is a fair number of years to sift through. If there are any inaccuracies in the times, names, or events that are described in this book—it is our leap of faith that the good intentions behind this project will outweigh any possible errors on the part of either author.

One tenth of the profits from this book will be donated annually to SHARE's orphan sponsorship program. Anyone interested in sponsoring a SHARE orphan can do so through SHARE's web site at www.shareafrica.org.

One last note to my sons, James and Jesse—believe in your dreams and follow your heart. You will get what you give. Put your best out there for the world to see. Live life to its fullest and make a difference along the way. Do it for you, and do it for Reid, Rob, and Scott—who never had the chance to.

Love you,

Mom

To Bobby,
Thank you from the bottom of my heart for allowing me to walk with you on your journey. It has given me more than I ever expected and even more than I could have ever hoped for.
Much love for you always,
Lynn

To God,
Thank you for this life, and for perfect timing. Thank you for difficulties that turn into blessings. And thank you for knowing better than me. I look forward to what comes next.
With boundless love,
Lynn

About the Authors

Dr. Martha MacGuffie, Bobby as she preferred, was a plastic and reconstructive surgeon, mother, grandmother, great grandmother, sister, friend, animal lover, activist, humanitarian, tireless octogenarian, excellent role model, teacher, and a force to be reckoned with. At the time of this writing she resided in Rockland County, New York, in the home that she loved with her faithful furry companion Teddy.

Lynn Cluess Manzione is a mother, wife, daughter, sister, friend, photographer, writer, promoter of positive role models, volunteer, student, teacher, and, since meeting Bobby ... evolving into more. At the time of this writing she resided a few miles away from her good friend Bobby with her husband Gregg, their sons James and Jesse, and her favorite dog Pepper.

Bobby and SHARE Africa welcome your ideas and contributions

www.shareafrica.org

Made in the USA
San Bernardino, CA
05 February 2020

64054175R00134